New book releases are free the first 48 hours. Every month, there is a free download on Kindle. To know of new releases and dates for free downloads, please subscribe at

www.TessaCason.com

Tessa Cason
5694 Mission Ctr. Rd. #602-213
San Diego, CA. 92108
www.TessaCason.com
Tessa@TessaCason.com

© Tessa Cason, Little Sage Enterprises, LLC, 2022.

LEGAL NOTICE AND DISCLAIMER:

From author and publisher: The information in this book is not intended to diagnose or treat any particular disease and/or condition. Nothing contained herein is meant to replace qualified medical or psychological advice and/or services. The author and publisher do not assume responsibility for how the reader chooses to apply the techniques herein. Use of the information is at the reader's discretion and discernment. The author and publisher specifically disclaim any and all liability arising directly or indirectly from the use or application contained in this book.

Nothing contained in this book is to be considered medical advice for any specific situation. This information is not intended as a substitute for the advice or medical care of a Physician prior to taking any personal action with respect to the information contained in this book. This book and all of its contents are intended for educational and informational purpose only. The information in this book is believed to be reliable, but is presented without guaranty or warranty.

By reading further, you agree to release the author and publisher from any damages or injury associated with your use of the material in this book.

700 EFT Tapping Statements™ for Weight, Emotional Eating, and Food Cravings

Tessa Cason, MA

My EFT Tapping Story

I established a life coaching practice in 1996 when life coaching was in its infancy. After several years, I realized that desire, exploration, and awareness did not equate to change and transformation for my clients.

Exploring the underlying cause of their pain, knowing their motivation to change, and defining who they wanted to become, did not create the changes in their lives they desired.

My livelihood was depended on the success of my clients. I realized I needed a tool or technique or method to aid my clients in their quest for change.

At the time, I knew that everything in our lives, all of our thoughts and feelings, choices and decisions, habits and experiences, actions and reactions were the result of our beliefs.

I knew that the beliefs were "stored" in our subconscious mind.

I knew that to transform and change our lives, we needed to heal the underlying unhealthy, dysfunctional beliefs on the subconscious level. I needed a tool, technique, or method to eliminate and heal the beliefs stored in the subconscious mind.

I visited a friend who managed a bookstore and told her of my dilemma, that I needed something to help my clients truly change and transform their lives. She reached for a book on the counter, near the register. "People have been raving about this book on EFT, Emotional Freedom Technique. Try it and see if it can help your clients."

In the 1990s, the internet was not an everyday part of our lives. Popular books sold more by word of mouth than any other means. Managing a bookstore, my friend knew what worked and what did not work. I trusted my friend, so I purchased the book.

As I read the book and discovered that EFT was tapping our head, I was unsure if this was the technique that would help my clients. I had some adventurous and forgiving clients whom I taught how to tap. When **every single client** returned for their next appointment and shared how different their lives had been that week because of tapping, I took notice! I was intrigued.

I learned that the first statement we needed to tap was: "It's not okay or safe for my life to change."

I learned that when a tapping statement did not clear, it meant there were other dysfunctional beliefs preventing the statement from clearing. When a statement didn't clear, I turned the statement into a question.

I learned that for EFT Tapping to work, we needed to find the cause of an issue.

I learned that clearing an emotional memory was different from clearing dysfunctional beliefs.

I learned that tapping one side of the body was more effective that tapping both sides simultaneously.

Clients started asking for tapping homework. I wrote out statements for them to tap. Soon, I had a library of tapping statements on different emotional issues.

I have been an EFT Practitioner since 2000. Working with hundreds of clients, one-on-one, I learned how to successfully utilize EFT so my clients could grow and transform their lives.

TABLE OF CONTENTS

Chapter 1
Intro

The identity of a person with excess weight is 'I'm a fat person.' This individual may diet and lose weight in the short term, but they will always gain it back. Their sense of certainty about who they are will guide their behaviors until the self is once again consistent with their identity. If the identity is that of a fat person, they will regain the weight to fulfill that identity. The self will fulfill our beliefs about ourselves, even when they are destructive and disempowering.

Tony Robbins

Overweight and obesity rates have increased dramatically in the last 30 years and are expected to continue to increase year after year. More than three out of four Americans are overweight (74%, according to the Center for Disease Control and Prevention). Globally, 39% of the population is overweight. The weight loss industry is a $200+ billion-dollar industry—and still, obesity is on the rise.

The usual weight loss programs aren't working. Huge clue: Approximately 95% of people who lose weight put it right back on.

Though billions of dollars are spent each year to heal the obesity issue, it still persists. The reason? Weight is the symptom. Not the cause. Not the issue. The usual programs for weight loss aren't working because they are attempting to solve the problem by dealing with the symptom, instead of healing the cause.

There are several reasons why we overeat and are overweight. We eat:

* For comfort,
* To numb out,
* Out of boredom,
* For pleasure,
* To stuff feelings,
* To suppress feelings,
* For a reward,
* For love,
* And the list goes on...

These reasons are symptoms. Not the cause.

* Overeating is a symptom.
* Eating until we are stuffed is a symptom.
* Eating to suppress our emotions is a symptom.
* Eating to numb out is a symptom.

Excess weight, food cravings, emotional eating, and overeating are symptoms of deeper, unresolved issues beneath the weight. Attempting to solve the problem by only dealing with the symptoms is ineffective and does not heal the issue.

One of the deeper issues beneath the weight is self-love. The lack of self-love and the shame that we may not be lovable or good enough to be loved is one cause. The result is excess weight, overeating, and emotional eating.

During World War II, babies in orphanages died, even though they received enough food. Their death was the result of not being loved, held, touched, comforted, and/or stroked. As infants, to survive, we are dependent upon others to love, comfort, stroke, and hold us.

For survival, when we don't love ourselves, we are dependent on others to show us love and to make us feel loved, lovable, and accepted. If we don't believe that we are lovable, will we believe that anyone else would find us lovable? If someone did find us lovable, would we believe them? If they found us lovable, would we question their judgment or maybe their intent?

If the various weight loss programs haven't healed the obesity issue, acknowledging the problem has not healed the obesity issue, having an ah-ha awareness hasn't healed the obesity issue, and talk therapy hasn't healed the obesity issue, how do we heal the obesity issue?

Great question.

Beliefs precede all of our thoughts, feeling, decisions, choices, habits, and experiences. To change our lives, we need to change our beliefs that cause the issue.

> If we want to heal our weight issues, we need to heal the cause...
> the dysfunctional beliefs and emotions beneath the symptom.

Excess Weight:

Cause – Lack of self-love and shame that we are not lovable or good enough to be loved.

Result – Overeating; eating to suppress emotions...to suppress anger, grief, and hurt; dependence on others to show us love, to make us feel lovable and that we are good enough to be loved.

How do we learn to love ourselves?

To heal our weight issues, we must learn how to be intimate with ourselves
and release the dysfunctional beliefs that prevent us from doing so.

We begin by examining our lives. To change our lives, we must recognize, acknowledge, and take ownership of our issues to be able to heal.

When we examine our lives, we will be able to identify the dysfunctional beliefs that contribute to and/or cause our emotional eating, overeating, and not eating foods that nourish the body.

THE POWER OF THREE

Issues that are difficult to heal seem to have at least two emotions that are "locked" together with the issue. To heal and clear an issue, all facets of the issue need to be cleared together, at the same time.

THE LOCKED IN EMOTIONS WITH WEIGHT ARE ANGER AND GRIEF.

If we want to heal our weight issues, we need to heal the cause...the dysfunctional beliefs and emotions.

Once we can identify the dysfunctional beliefs, these beliefs need to be deleted on a subconscious level. There is a powerful tool called EFT tapping that can do just that—change beliefs on a subconscious level.

EFT Tapping is a very powerful tool that can help us transform our lives forever.

Food Cravings

Our food cravings are trying to tell us something, and it's not about the foods.

* Craving sweets might indicate a lack of joy in our lives.
* Craving crunchy foods might be an indication of the frustration that we are feeling.
* Craving bread might be an attempt to fill the emptiness in our lives.

Food cravings are symptoms. They are not the issue. Food cravings are symptoms of deeper issues in our lives. They are indications of what we need to heal.

THE ONLY WAY TO TRULY END FOOD CRAVINGS IS TO HEAL THE CAUSE.

To heal our food cravings, we must recognize, acknowledge, address, desensitize, and/or delete the thoughts, emotions, and memories that propel us toward the foods that we crave.

Healing begins with an awareness of our actions and an understanding of the triggers that lead to the action. Knowing the significance of our food cravings can provide insights into what we really are craving.

TO HEAL OUR FOOD CRAVINGS, WE NEED TO HEAL THE UNDERLYING CAUSE... OUR DYSFUNCTIONAL BELIEFS AND EMOTIONS.

Anger

Anger is one of the bottom lines of overweight, overeating, and emotional eating.

Anger and frustration are natural emotions. Anger is not in itself right or wrong, healthy or unhealthy, appropriate or inappropriate. It is the *expression* of anger that makes it right or wrong, healthy or unhealthy, appropriate or inappropriate. Unhealthy anger is when anger is directed toward another to be hurtful and do harm. Wrong and inappropriate anger is when anger is violent and used to punish, intimidate, control, and manipulate.

Anger that is repressed and aggressive is unhealthy anger. It is unhealthy to stuff, ignore, and/or pretend the anger does not exist.

* RESENTMENT is unexpressed anger.

* PASSIVE-AGGRESSIVE ANGER is anger meant to inflict pain.

* RAGE is abusive anger filled with feelings of fear, sadness, shame, inadequacy, guilt, and/or loss.

*DEPRESSION is anger that we think we would get in trouble for having, thus depressing the anger.

*GUILT is anger that we don't feel we have a right to have.

* APATHY is suppressed anger.

*WORRY is anticipated anger.

*ANXIETY is a combination of four things: UNIDENTIFIED ANGER, HURT, FEAR, AND/OR SELF-PITY.

©Tessa Cason, 2021.

Grief

Another bottom line of overweight, overeating, and emotional eating is grief.

Grief is more than sadness. It is more than unhappiness. Grief is a loss. Something of value is gone. Grief is an intense loss that breaks our hearts. Loss can be the death of a loved one, a way of life, a job, a marriage, or one's own imminent death. Grief is real.

Grief has many faces. Grief can show up as:

* Pain
* Hurt
* Shame
* Apathy
* Regret
* Depression
* Loneliness
* Hopelessness
* Disillusionment
* Disappointment
* Feeling unloved
* Feeling rejected
* Shattered dreams
* Feeling overwhelmed
* Feeling that we don't belong
* Feeling that life and our life is meaningless

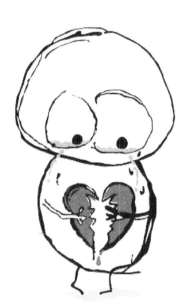

Over time, unhealed grief becomes anger, blame, resentment, righteousness, and/or remorse. We become someone whom we are not. It takes courage to move through the grief and all the emotions buried deep within. The depth of our pain is an indication of the importance and significance something has for us.

* How has your life been limited by your weight? A romantic relationship? A job and/or a promotion at work?
* Has your weight prevented you from living the life that you thought you would be living?
* Has your weight prevented you from having the marriage and/ or family that you desired?
* Do you avoid doing a specific activity because of your weight?
* Do you have the energy needed to fulfill your wish?

WHAT HAVE YOU LOST AS A RESULT OF THE EXCESS WEIGHT YOU CARRY AROUND DAY AFTER DAY AFTER DAY?

Elisabeth Kubler-Ross developed five states of grief. These states are not sequential. They may coexist with other states, be skipped completely, occur intermittently, or repeat themselves. She believed that grief is a continuously evolving process that offers potential for growth.

The states are: Denial, Anger, Bargaining, Depression, and Acceptance.

The Grand Canyon was not punished by windstorms over hundreds of years. In fact, it was created by them. We are a creation with the unbelievable power to weather life's toughest storms. If someone had tried to shield the Grand Canyon from the windstorm, we would never have the beauty of its carvings.

Elisabeth Kubler-Ross and David

Not Good Enough

When we don't love ourselves, we feel that we are not good enough.

Feeling not good enough or "less than" is played out in a cycle of shame, hopelessness, and self-pity. We feel shame about who we are, that we have little value, and that we are not good enough. Feeling "less than" spirals down into depression, self-sabotage, and survival.

Not being good enough creates an illusion of fear—fear of being rejected, abandoned, left out, and/or forgotten.

Feeling not good enough, less than, sorry for ourselves, and hopeless keep us stuck in survival. When in survival, it is risky to step outside of our comfort zone. Thus, the pattern repeats itself over and over.

When we feel less than and not good enough, our self-worth and self-esteem are lacking. Self-esteem is the ability to earn love. When self-esteem is lacking, we lack self-respect, pride, and self-love.

When we don't feel good enough, we lack self-love and self-esteem. We don't love ourselves, and we cannot earn love. The result? Anger, frustration, grief, self-pity, hurt, shame, apathy, helplessness, and hopelessness...

Failure

* Failure is about LACK. Lack of power, persistence, courage, confidence, skills, knowledge, talent, etc.
* Failure is about the willingness to stay stuck in hopelessness and helplessness.
* Failure is giving up and feeling that this is the best it will ever be.

The opposite of failure is success. By examining what successful people do, we might be able to determine where our failure occurs, or at least, what is contributing to our failure.

Even though success is different for each of us, there are common threads throughout all successes. Here are some of the common threads:

Successful people:

* Take action.
* Focus on solutions and are solution-oriented.
* Make decisions and continue to move forward.
* Are flexible about the process of achieving their goals.
* Know that life is not a rehearsal for something else.
* Have a detailed plan to accomplish their goals and dreams.
* Understand that setbacks and obstacles will teach them valuable lessons.
* Know everything that they accomplish in life is up to them.
* Understand there is no guarantee that they will succeed.
* Understand the seeds that they plant today will be the rewards that they harvest tomorrow.
* Expect to meet many obstacles and difficulties along the way.
* Know that failure is only temporary, just part of the process.
* Take complete responsibility for their lives.
* Set goals and work toward their fulfillment.
* Accept change and adapt to difficulties.
* Pick themselves up after failure and press on.
* Are resilient and persistent.
* Don't quit or give up.
* Are willing to accept feedback and self-correct.
* Live in the "now," present in their lives.
* Know what they want.

Chapter 2
Emma's Story

As the sun sets, Emma helps Olivia, her younger sister, and Tom, her future brother-in-law, carry the last of the shower gifts to their vehicle. She waves goodbye from her front door, slips back inside, and collapses on the couch. As Emma surveys her living room, she sees wrapping paper, ribbon, and paper plates from the couple's wedding shower scattered throughout the room.

Slowly, the smile on Emma's face melts away and tears begin to fill her eyes. Tonight, at the couple's wedding shower, she was the only person who was "dateless." Easy enough to make excuses when you are the hostess and need to focus on the bride and her guests. Truthfully, there is no one special in Emma's life.

As Olivia's maid of honor, the last six months have been all about weddings...wedding shows, wedding dresses, wedding venues, wedding photographers...the list goes on. She loves her sister. They are best friends. As children, each went on and on about their weddings. She wants to help Olivia plan this very special day.

Olivia's wedding is now a reality. And Emma's? Emma gave up on finding Mr. Right a long time ago. After graduating from college sixteen years ago, the flow of dates began trickling down from a few per year to now nil. None. Like, zero. Emma hasn't gone on a date in years.

The date of Olivia's wedding is fast approaching. What that means for Emma is seeing long-time family friends who she hasn't seen in a long time. There will be questions, "And you, Emma, have you found Mr. Right? Are you dating? How's the diet going?"

Dreading the embarrassment, tears spill down Emma's face. Her heart quickens, as her anxiety level increases. Mrs. Erickson, the next-door neighbor and town gossip, had RSVPed her attendance. Oh, and Mrs. Carter, her three daughters, and their spouses all RSVPed "yes," as well. All three of the Carter daughters are younger than Emma!

At the wedding, Emma would be dateless, again. To be "polite," both Mrs. Erickson and Mrs. Carter will start a conversation with Emma. She might as well wear a sign that says, "No, I'm not married. No, I'm not dating. And yes, I'm on a diet."

Emma lacks the energy and the motivation to clean up after the couple's wedding shower. "Tomorrow," she thinks. "Tomorrow, I'll clean up." Emma had taken the week off work so she could host the shower for her sister. "Tomorrow, I'll sleep and then clean up."

Emma lets out a weary, heavy sigh. All of Olivia's dreams have come true. Olivia is a natural with a camera. She can easily put people at ease and is now a highly sought-after portrait photographer. After seeing Olivia's work, Tom contacted Olivia to ask if she wanted to do a show in his gallery. Their meeting was one of those magical moments that you see in the movies. This isn't the movies though. This is real life.

Thinking about her own passions and dreams, Emma lets out another huge sigh. Children were Emma's passion. She was a natural with children. Growing up, she was everyone's go-to babysitter. As a child, she knew that children would be a part of her life as an adult. She wanted a house full of children and a career as a therapist for children.

Well, life didn't work out as Emma thought it would. No husband. No house full of children. No career as a therapist for children. And, still overweight.

Emma's major in college was nursing with a minor in child development. After graduating from college, Emma was hired at the local hospital. When she decided to become a nurse, Emma imagined creating bonds with her patients. She wanted to help those who were unable to help themselves. Looking back now, she realizes that she had an idealistic view of nursing. In reality, her days are spent rushing from room to room, dispersing meds, fluffing pillows, and taking orders from doctors.

Still unable to move from the couch, bemoaning her less-than-ideal life, her cell phone rings. Emma pulls her phone out of her pocket, checks the caller ID, and decides to answer.

"Good evening, Hannah," says Emma with no pretense in her voice. Hannah's and Emma's moms are sisters. Even though Hannah and Emma are cousins, they feel more like sisters, only ten months apart in age. No need for pretense.

"Whoa! Did the couple's wedding shower go badly? You sound horrible. What's going on, dear cousin? Talk to me," demands Hannah.

"I was the only person who was at the shower alone, stag, dateless. Even if you were here, you and Stephen would have been another couple at the couple's wedding shower!" says Emma.

"So, you are depressed because you were dateless tonight?" asks Hannah, a little confused. "Did something happen at the shower?"

"The shower went well. Everyone had a great time," Emma says.

"Nothing happened at the shower to trigger this depression?" asks Hannah doubtfully.

Emma lets out a sigh and says, "I've been glued to the couch ever since the shower ended an hour ago. Olivia's dream of being a wife is coming true. I've been comparing the outcome of my life to my sister's. And I don't understand how I got here, and she got there, how all of her dreams came true and none of mine did."

"It also sounds like you have been crying and maybe crying right now," comments Hannah.

Pulling out a tissue from her pocket, Emma blows her nose and responds, "True. I was sitting here feeling sorry for myself and crying."

With compassion, Hannah asks Emma if she wants to share what is going on.

"Oh, Hannah," Emma starts. "With Olivia's engagement, the last six months have been everything wedding. Wedding dresses. Wedding shows. Wedding venues. I'm happy for Olivia, that she has met such a wonderful man who adores her. Seeing Olivia so happy, I feel the void in my life."

Emma continues, "Remember, as kids we would dream about what our lives would be like one day? Well, your dreams came true. And now Olivia's dreams are coming true, too. I'm sad that my dreams never came true. There is no hope of my dreams coming true."

"Not a fun place to be, in grief," says Hannah with understanding. She knows better than to offer solutions or insights.

Feeling dejected and hopeless, Emma says, "I am a failure. My life looks good on the outside, but I'm miserable on the inside. I don't know how to do my life any differently than I am. I know. I know you have wanted to share with me how you turned your life around, and how you were able to achieve your dreams. I know you have wanted to have a talk with me for months. Or has it been years?"

"I did find some answers for myself," Hannah says, secretly hoping that Emma is finally ready to hear about her transformation.

"Hannah, you have always had your life together. You were destined to be successful," Emma says.

"I didn't have my life together, Emma. I was a mess!" remarks Hannah. "Destined to be successful? Emma, success doesn't just happen. It takes work."

"Oh, Hannah, I didn't mean to diminish the work you have done. I know you have worked hard for your success. Is there hope for me? You've known me my whole life. If anyone would know if there were hope for me, it would be you," Emma says with sadness in her voice.

With laughter, Hannah comments, "Knowing you as I do, I can say with certainty that there's hope and a tremendous amount of potential in you!"

Emma asks, "Do you have time tomorrow to talk?"

"As a matter of fact," says Hannah, "I don't have any classes that I have to teach tomorrow. So, yes, I have time tomorrow to talk." They agree on a time and then say goodnight to each other.

To unwind from the craziness of the day and the wedding shower, Emma decides to take a warm bath with lots of bubbles. As she slips into the water, tears roll down her face.

Emma has struggled with her weight for 25 years. "25 years!" thinks Emma. "I started dieting in high school, and I'm still overweight! I can see now how I overate back then, in high school. Olivia was the baby and very pretty. Harry was the oldest and a great athlete. And then, there was me. Ordinary in every way. Nothing special. It seemed that Harry and Olivia were showered with attention. I felt as if I were invisible and didn't matter."

"And I know why I overeat now—to fill the void and soothe the disappointment. I know all of that, but I still overeat. How sad is that?" asks Emma of herself.

Emma feels her anxiety and panic kick in. "I'm 38 years old! It's too late to have children. Need a man, preferably a husband, to complete the equation of children. No husband on the horizon. No man even in the vicinity!" thinks Emma.

Everything feels hopeless. "I am so uncomfortable around men because of my weight. Do I really want a man who would want this overweight body? To become a therapist, I must go back to school. Once I finish school, I would have to apply for a position. Well, that just sent my anxiety through the roof! Besides," thinks Emma, "who would hire an old, overweight therapist?"

"I'm too worn out tonight to think anymore. I'll let Hannah sort it out for me." With this thought, Emma dries off, puts on her pajamas, and climbs into bed.

At the appointed time the next day, Hannah calls Emma. Emma answers the phone and says, "Before you ask, yes, I want to hear your story of transformation. And, yes, I want help figuring out my transformation. I do have to warn you, my anxiety is climbing just talking about transformation."

"Do you think that you are ready to let your anxiety go, too?" asks Hannah.

"What do you mean, let it go? I've been anxious my whole life. It's not something that you just let go," responds Emma.

Hannah starts, "Emma, if you could change one thing about your life, what would it be?"

Without hesitation, Emma quickly responds, "My weight."

Hannah asks why her weight.

"Simple. If I lost the weight, I wouldn't feel like a loser, feel less than everyone else. I would be comfortable dating. Oh, and I wouldn't be anxious about applying for a therapist job."

"Whoa! A lot of pressure is tied to weight. So, I guess your weight has you waiting to live your life," comments Hannah.

"My weight has me waiting to live my life? Wait. Weight. Oh, I get it. I guess so. Don't get me wrong, I like my life," responds Emma.

"You like your life. Are you happy?" asks Hannah.

Hearing the questions, tears flow down Emma's cheek and she is unable to speak.

Hannah says, "The silence from your end of the phone is deadening!"

Emma is still unable to respond.

With gentleness, Hannah says, "Emma, maybe it's not about the weight at all. Maybe moving forward with your life, or fulfilling your dreams, or being a wife, maybe it's easy to point the finger at your weight and allow this to stop you from moving forward."

In between sniffles, Emma comments, "What if I lost the weight and no man wanted me? What if I did all the training required to be a therapist for children and I suck at it? What if I had a house full of children and I couldn't manage a husband, children, career, friends, and all the other requirements of my life?"

"Emma," says Hannah, "that's a lot of 'what ifs.' Every one of those sentences started with 'what if' as if life happens to you."

"But life does happen, whether we want it to or not. We are truly powerless to create the life that we want," says Emma with surety.

"I respectfully disagree, Emma," says Hannah. "I used to think that life happened to me until I realized that I could create the reality I wanted."

"I guess that was the beginning of your transformation," says Emma.

"Yes. I attended a conference. One of the speakers was an EFT practitioner. EFT stands for Emotional Freedom Technique. From the stage, she led the whole audience through tapping."

"I've heard of tapping," says Emma, quizzically. "Tapping your head is what transformed your life?"

"I would never have tried tapping on my own," says Hannah. "I tapped with the group at the conference. The immediate changes that I felt after tapping...I couldn't contribute the feelings to anything else other than the tapping. I was intrigued. Later in the day, I approached the speaker, the EFT practitioner. I decided to do sessions with her to clear out the anxiety and 'what ifs' that our family is known for. Now, when I am tempted to do the 'what if' thing, I tap. The 'what if' is the excuse for not moving forward with my life. Tapping allows me to figure out the fear that I have of moving forward into the unknown."

"I don't understand what tapping has to do with losing weight. Tapping my head and the weight will melt away?" asks Emma.

"Emma," Hannah says cautiously, "maybe the weight is only a symptom. Over the years, I've heard about the diets, the exercises, and everything else that you have done to lose weight. Do you think that maybe the reason you haven't lost the weight is because it's not about what you eat or how much you exercise?"

"How could it not be about what I eat or exercising?" asks Emma. "I really am trying to understand, but I don't. What I do know is that nothing will change in my life until I lose the weight. My weight stops me from everything. I can't find love because of my weight. I can't really be happy until I lose weight. I can't have fun because of my weight. I can't do anything because of my weight, and yes, that includes starting a new career," Emma sighs.

"Understanding ourselves, our motives, and our needs is complex," says Hannah. "We are not one-dimensional. We are multi-faceted beings. I just emailed you the website of my EFT practitioner. If you have any interest, take a look. She has lots of different blogs that explain everything much better than I can."

Later that evening, Emma pulls up the website. Before she knows it, two hours have gone by. After she reads glowing testimonials, watches several tapping videos, and listens to the EFT practitioner's weight loss story, Emma is intrigued. The practitioner, Lucy, offers a free 15-minute session. Emma, out of respect for her cousin, schedules a 15-minute appointment with Lucy.

Again, Emma's anxiety ramps up as the appointment approaches. She has never worked with a therapist before and feels that only those people who have serious problems need a therapist. If she works with Lucy, it means that she has serious problems and that increases her anxiety even more!

When Lucy answers the phone, she asks if she is speaking to Emma. "Yes, this is Emma," Emma says.

"Good. In your email, you said that you and Hannah are cousins. I am very proud of the transformation that Hannah was able to achieve. When that woman decides that she wants something, she puts her whole heart and soul into whatever it is she wants," says Lucy.

"Yup. That's my cousin. We used to tease her as kids and called her 'Headstrong Hannah'!" says Emma.

"Emma, we have 15 minutes today, "says Lucy. "What would you like to get accomplished in this time? What are you wanting to change in your life? Or what is it about your life that you don't enjoy?"

"My weight. Can you help me lose weight?" asks Emma. "I am under a little bit of a time crunch. My sister is getting married soon. I'm the maid of honor. I know that I can't lose all the weight that I need to lose before then, but if I can lose a little bit of weight, that would be great."

"Let me ask you a question," says Lucy. "What does the excess weight prevent you from doing? What do you avoid doing because of your weight?"

"Interesting question. Hannah asked me something similar. I've thought about her question for the last couple of weeks," says Emma.

"Did you come up with an answer?" asks Lucy.

"I think so. Maybe. I'm not sure," says Emma with reservation.

"What is the answer that you arrived at?" asks Lucy.

Speaking slowly, Emma says, "I guess that I avoid anything and everything that makes me anxious and nervous, which is just about everything."

Lucy asks Emma if she could be specific.

Emma responds, "Well, dating, going back to school, pursuing my dream job."

"How do you feel about dating?" asks Lucy.

"Frightened," replies Emma.

"How do you feel about going back to school?" asks Lucy.

"Frightened," says Emma. "And next, you are going to ask me how I feel about pursuing my dream job. The answer will be 'frightened,' the same as the first two."

"Then is it about the weight and/or something else? Could it be about fear? Could fear be the cause and the weight the distraction from facing the fear?" says Lucy slowly.

Thinking, taking it all in, Emma responds, "So, you are saying that I'm fat to keep myself safe from doing things that frighten me?"

Lucy responds, "Maybe the weight is a symptom. Maybe the weight is not the cause. Let's say that you are riding a bike. The tire goes flat. You keep putting air in the tire, but the tire still goes flat. Is the tire flat because it doesn't have air in it, or does the tire go flat because there is a nail in it?"

"Both would be true, correct?" asks Emma.

"Yes, both are true. What is the ultimate cause?" asks Lucy.

"The nail?" answers Emma, unsure.

"Maybe your weight is the lack of air in the tire. Maybe your fear is the nail that causes the tire to lose air," adds Lucy.

"I'm not sure that I understand. Weight isn't about what I eat or how much I exercise?" asks Emma. "It's about the nail in the tire? I'm lost."

"Let me ask you this, Emma. Earlier, you said that you knew you overate as a child because you felt invisible and didn't matter. And now, as an adult, you overeat to fill the void and soothe the disappointment. Correct?" asks Lucy.

"Correct," responds Emma. "I also eat when I am anxious. And I'm anxious a lot! I mean a lot!"

"How would your life look if you could heal the anxiety?" asks Lucy.

Puzzled, Emma asks, "Heal the anxiety? I didn't know that you could heal anxiety."

Lucy says, "Anxiety is a combination of four things: unidentified anger, hurt, fear, and self-pity. We expect error, rejection, and humiliation...and actually start to anticipate it."

"Oh, so feeling that everything is hopeless fuels my anxiety," says Emma slowly, thinking.

"Exactly! Meeting men frightens you. Could it be that you are possibly expecting rejection?" asks Lucy.

"Ms. Lucy, I think that I need some help! I never thought that my anxiety was something that could be healed. I am so tired of the anxiety. I am so tired of this excess weight! When can we begin?" asks an excited Emma.

Laughing, Lucy says, "Whenever you want!"

"Like a year ago. I have a wedding, and I want to knock the socks off a few people!" exclaims Emma.

Week after week, Lucy expertly guides Emma in uncovering and clearing the unresolved emotions and beliefs that created the need to hold onto the excess weight, along with her anxiety. She discovers that her anxiety and fears were merely a result of the belief that she was "less than." Believing that she was less than everyone else, she feared rejection. Fear of rejection generated a tidal wave of anxiety.

Some of what Emma dealt with and healed from was her:

* Anger that she didn't get the love and attention that she needed as a child.
* Anger that her life had not turned out the way that she wanted.
* Self-pity that everyone else had it easier than her.
* Fear of change, rejection, and being judged.
* Shame of being single, overweight, not good enough, and feeling like a failure and loser.

Emma experienced incredible shifts and changes in her life as she processed her anxiety and felt "less than."

Emma was dateless for her sister's wedding, and that was okay with Emma. She had lost weight before the wedding and felt great in her beautiful maid of honor gown. She handled Mrs. Erickson and Mrs. Carter with ease and actually enjoyed chatting with everyone at the wedding. She was applauded for the maid of honor toast and speech that she gave. To her great surprise, she was asked out on several dates with some very handsome, intelligent men who were also dateless at the wedding.

After some research, Emma decided to enroll in a training course to earn her certification in play therapy for children. She became a certified EFT practitioner to incorporate EFT into her therapy with children.

A year after beginning her work with Lucy, Emma sent Hannah flowers with a note that said, "Thank you." Upon receiving the flowers, Hannah pulled out her cell phone and called Emma. Emma answered the phone by saying, "Thank you."

"Emma, I am so proud of you for transforming your life and creating the reality you want!" said Hannah with excitement. "In this last year, you started courses in earning a certification to fulfill your dream of working with children. You've been dating David, a great guy by the way, ever since Olivia's wedding. You slimmed down to your ideal weight. And I can hear the happiness in your voice."

With gratitude, Emma said, "With your persistence and support, EFT tapping, and Lucy, I have been able to transform the anxiety and feeling of less than into joy and fulfillment. Thank you for being you! Thank you for loving me and being my guide and shining example!"

EFT TAPPING

Chapter 3
EFT Tapping – Emotional Freedom Technique

EFT Tapping is a very easy technique to learn. It involves making a statement as we contact the body by either circling or tapping.

An EFT Tapping Statement has three parts:

Part 1: starts with "**Even though**" followed by

Part 2: a statement which could be the **dysfunctional emotion or belief**, and

Part 3: ends with "**I totally and completely accept myself.**"

A complete statement would be, "**Even though I fear change, I totally and completely accept myself.**"

Instruction for the Short Form of EFT Tapping

The instructions below are for using the right hand. Reverse the directions to tap using the left hand. It is more effective, when we tap, to tap only one side rather than both.

I. SET UP – BEGIN WITH CIRCLING OR TAPPING THE SIDE OF THE HAND:

A. With the fingertips of the right hand, find a tender spot below the left collar bone. Once the tender spot is identified, press firmly on the spot, moving the fingertips in a circular motion toward the left shoulder, toward the outside, clockwise. Tapping the side of the hand can also be used instead of the circling.

B. As the fingers circle and press against the tender spot or tap the side of the hand, repeat the tapping statement three times: "Even though,___[tapping statement]___, I totally and completely accept myself." An example would be: "Even though I fear change, I totally and completely accept myself."

Side of the hand

Tender spot below the left collar bone

II. TAPPING:

A. After the third time, tap the following eight points, repeating the [tapping statement] at each point. Tap each point five – ten times:

1. The inner edge of the eyebrow, just above the eye. [I fear change.]
2. Temple, just to the side of the eye. [I fear change.]
3. Just below the eye (on the cheekbone). [I fear change.]
4. Under the nose. [I fear change.]
5. Under the lips. [I fear change.]
6. Under the knob of the collar bone. [I fear change.]
7. Three inches under the arm pit. [I fear change.]
8. Top back of the head. [I fear change.]

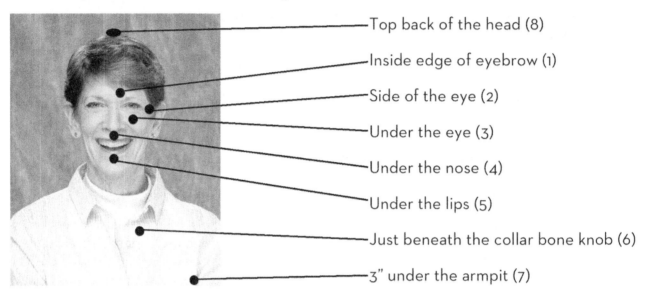

Top back of the head (8)

Inside edge of eyebrow (1)

Side of the eye (2)

Under the eye (3)

Under the nose (4)

Under the lips (5)

Just beneath the collar bone knob (6)

3" under the armpit (7)

B. After tapping, take a deep breath. If you are not able to take a deep, full, satisfying breath, do eye rolls.

III. EYE ROLLS

A. With one hand tap continuously on the **back** of the other hand between the fourth and fifth fingers.
B. Hold your head straight forward, eyes looking straight down.
C. For six seconds, roll your eyes from the floor straight up toward the ceiling while repeating the tapping statement. Keep the head straight forward, only moving the eyes.

IV. TAKE ANOTHER DEEP BREATH.

Chapter 4
EFT Tapping, Beliefs, and the Subconscious Mind

EFT - Emotional Freedom Technique

EFT is a technique that allows us to change dysfunctional beliefs and emotions on a subconscious level. It involves making a statement while tapping different points along meridian paths.

The general principle behind EFT is that the cause of all negative emotions is a disruption in the body's energy system. By tapping on locations where several different meridians flow, we can release unproductive memories, emotions, and beliefs that cause the blockages.

A Belief is...

A belief is a mental acceptance of, and conviction in, the Truth, actuality, or validity of something. It is what we believe to be true, whether it is Truth or not. A belief is a thought that influences energy all the time.

A Dysfunctional Belief is...

A dysfunctional belief is a belief that takes us away from peace, love, joy, stability, acceptance, and harmony. It causes us to feel stressed, fearful, anxious, and/or insecure.

The Conscious Mind is...

The conscious mind is the part of us that thinks, passes judgments, makes decisions, remembers, analyzes, has desires, and communicates with others. It is responsible for logic and reasoning, understanding and comprehension. The mind determines our actions, feelings, thoughts, judgments, and decisions **based on beliefs.**

The Subconscious Mind is...

The subconscious is the part of the mind responsible for all our involuntary actions like our heartbeat and breathing rate. It does not evaluate, make decisions, or pass judgment. It just is. It does not determine if something is "right" or "wrong."

The subconscious is much like the software of a computer. On the computer keyboard, if we press the key for the letter "a," we will see the letter "a" on the screen, even though we may have wanted to see "t." Just as a computer can only do what it has been programmed to do, we can only do as we are programmed to do.

Our programming is determined by our beliefs. Beliefs and memories are "stored" in the subconscious.

THREE RULES OF THE SUBCONSCIOUS MIND

Three rules of the subconscious mind include:

1. Personal. It only understands "I," "me," "myself." First-person.

2. Positive. The subconscious does not hear the word "no." When you say, "I am not going to eat that piece of cake," the subconscious mind hears, "Yummm! Cake! I am going to eat a piece of that cake!"

3. Present time. Time does not exist for the subconscious. The only time it knows is "now," present time. "I'm going to start my diet tomorrow." "Tomorrow" never comes; thus, the diet never starts.

Beliefs precede all of our thoughts, feelings,
decisions, choices, actions, reactions,
and experiences...

Our beliefs and memories are stored
in the subconscious mind.

If we want to make changes in our lives,
we have to change the programming,
the dysfunctional beliefs in the subconscious.

Three rules of the Subconscious Mind:
Personal
Positive
Present time

Chapter 5
How Does EFT Tapping Work?

1. Acceptance: The last part of the tapping statement, we say, "I totally and completely accept myself." **Acceptance brings us into present time.** We can only heal if we are in present time.

2. Addresses the current dysfunctional beliefs on a subconscious level: To make changes in our lives, we have to change the dysfunctional beliefs on a subconscious level. The middle part of the tapping statements are the "instructions" for the subconscious. **To make changes in our lives, we only care what the subconscious hears.**

3. Pattern interrupt: Dysfunctional memories and/or beliefs block energy from flowing freely along the meridians. Tapping is a pattern interrupt that disrupts the flow of energy to allow our **body's own Infinite Wisdom to come forth for healing.** (Tapping both sides does not act as a pattern interrupt.)

4. Mis-direct: One role of the physical body is to protect us. When our hand is too close to a flame, our body automatically pulls our hand back to safety. An EFT Tapping statement that agrees with the current belief is more effective. The physical body is less likely to sabotage the tapping if it agrees with the current belief.

For the EFT Taping statement "I fear change":

* This statement appeases the physical body since it agrees with the current belief.
* The tapping disrupts the energy flow so our Truth can come forth.

The body will always gravitate to health, wealth, and well-being when the conditions allow it. EFT Tapping weeds the garden so the blossoms can bloom more easily and effortlessly.

Chapter 6
Benefits of Using EFT Tapping

* The last part of the statement is, "I totally and completely **accept** myself." **Acceptance** brings us into present time. Healing can only take place when we are in present time.

* By tapping, we are **calling forth our Truths.** The keyword here is "**our.**" Not anyone else's. If my name is "Lucas," tapping the statement "Even though my name is Troy," my name will not change to Troy.

* Tapping **calls forth our body's Infinite Wisdom.** When we cut our finger, our body knows how to heal the cut itself. Once the dysfunctional emotions, experiences, and beliefs have been "deleted," our body **automatically** gravitates to health, wealth, wisdom, peace, love, joy...

* By changing dysfunctional beliefs and emotions on a subconscious level, the changes we make with EFT are **permanent.**

* EFT Tapping can change:

Beliefs
Emotions
Self-images
Our story
Thoughts
Mind chatter
Painful memories

* EFT Tapping can neutralize stored memories that block energy along the meridians.

* EFT Tapping can desensitize emotions. We might have a difficult person in our life who ignores us and/or criticizes us, so we tap the statement: "This difficult person [or their name] ignores and criticizes me."

Tapping does not mean they will no longer ignore and/or criticize us; however, it can **desensitize us,** so we are no longer affected by their behavior. Once we have desensitized the emotions, our perception and mental thinking improve. We are better able to make informed decisions. We don't take and make everything personal. Our health is not negatively impacted. Our heart doesn't beat 100 beats/minute. Smoke stops coming out of our ears, and our faces don't turn red with anger and frustration.

Chapter 7
What We Say As We Tap Is VERY Important!

All of our beliefs are programmed into our subconscious minds. If we want to change our lives, we have to delete the dysfunctional beliefs on a subconscious level. The statements we make as we tap are the instructions for the subconscious mind.

THE TAPPING STATEMENTS WE WAY AS WE ARE TAPPING ARE CRITICAL FOR THIS TO HAPPEN!

Example: You get in a taxi. Several hours later, you still have not arrived at your destination. "*Why?*" you ask. Because you did not give the destination to the taxi driver!

Tapping without saying an adequate tapping statement is like riding in a cab without giving the cab driver our destination!

For EFT Tapping to be MOST EFFECTIVE the Tapping Statement is CRITICAL!

EFT Tapping allows us to delete the dysfunctional beliefs on a subconscious level. The statements we make as we tap are instructions to the subconscious mind so our Truth can come forth.

Chapter 8
Using a Negative EFT Tapping Statement

Our beliefs **precede** all of our thoughts, feelings, decisions, choices, actions, reactions, and experiences.

If we want to make changes in our lives, we have to change the dysfunctional beliefs. Our beliefs are stored in the subconscious.

To change our lives, to change a belief, we only care what the subconscious hears when we tap. The subconscious does not hear the word "no." When we say, "I am not going to eat that piece of cake," the subconscious hears, "Yummm, cake!"

Example, if we don't believe we have what it takes to be successful and we tap the statement, "I have what it takes to be successful," the body could sabotage the tapping. We could tap and it won't clear.

Instead, if the statement we make is, "I do not have what it takes to be successful," the "**not**" appeases the physical body and the subconscious hears, "I have what it takes to be successful!"

A tapping statement with the word "no" or "not" works best!

Chapter 9
EFT Tapping Statements Are Most Effective
When They Agree With Current Beliefs

The EFT Tapping statement is **more successful when** it **is something the body currently believes.**

*The body is less likely to sabotage
an EFT Tapping statement that
agrees with the current belief.*

One role of the physical body is to protect us from harm. (For example, if our hand gets too close to a flame, our body will pull our hand back to safety.) The body is less likely to sabotage the statement and the process if the EFT Tapping statement agrees with the current belief. Thus, it appeases the physical body.

For example, if our desire is prosperity and wealth and we tap the statement, "I am prosperous now," the body could sabotage the tapping by forgetting what we were saying, getting easily distracted, or our mind chatter may remind us we are not prosperous. We could tap and the statement, most likely, will not clear.

If the statement we say is "I am not prosperous now," the "**not**" appeases the physical body, and the subconscious hears, "I am prosperous now!"

Chapter 10
The Very First EFT Tapping Statement to Tap

The very first EFT Tapping statement I have clients and students tap is, "It is not okay or safe for my life to change." I have muscle tested this statement with more than a thousand people. Not one person tested strong that it was okay or safe for their life to change. (Muscle testing is a way in which we can converse with the body, bypassing the conscious mind.)

How effective can EFT or any
therapy be if it is not okay or safe
for our lives to change?

Since our lives are constantly changing, if it is not okay or safe for our lives to change, every time our lives change, it creates stress for the body. Stress creates another whole set of issues for ourselves, our lives, and our bodies.

Chapter 11
One Statement per Round of EFT vs
Multiple Statements per Round of EFT

Laser-focused Tapping vs Round Robin Tapping

Same Statement for all the Tapping Points in One Round
vs Multiple Statements in One Round of Tapping (Scripts)

Two styles of tapping for different purposes. One style is best for healing dysfunctional beliefs. The other style is best for healing emotions, desensitizing a story, situation, and/or memory.

I found that the laser-focused, one statement for a round of tapping was most effective for healing the beliefs. Multiple statements per round of tapping is great at healing emotions, desensitizing a story, situation, and/or memory.

SAME STATEMENT FOR ALL THE TAPPING POINTS IN ONE ROUND

After tapping the statement, "It's not okay for my life to change," and we are able to take a deep breath, we know the statement cleared. Then we tap, "I'm not ready for my life to change," and we are not able to take a deep breath, most likely, the statement did not clear.

Knowing the statement did not clear, we can focus on the reasons, excuses, and/or beliefs about not being ready to change our lives.

* Maybe the changes we need to make would require more of us than we want to give.
* Maybe we don't feel we have the abilities we would need if our life changed.
* Maybe we don't feel our support system, the people in our life, would support the changes we want to make.

Follow-up tapping statements for "I'm not ready for my life to change" could be:

* I do not have the abilities change would require.
* I am afraid of change.
* Others will not support the changes I want to make in my life.
* I am not able to make the changes I want to make.
* I do not have the courage that change would require.
* I am too old to change.

Tapping the same statement at all eight points is most effective for clearing beliefs. When a statement does not clear, we can focus on the reasons, excuses, and/or dysfunctional beliefs that blocked the statement from clearing.

MULTIPLE STATEMENTS IN ONE ROUND OF TAPPING (SCRIPTS/ROUND ROBIN)

Tapping multiple statements in one round, also known as Scripts or Round Robin tapping, is excellent for healing a story, and desensitizing a memory or story.

Healing a broken heart, to desensitize the heartache of the break up, the following script/ statements could be said, one statement/point:

* My boyfriend broke up with me.
* I am heartbroken.
* He said he doesn't love me anymore.
* I do not know how I can go on without him.
* It hurts.
* I am sad he doesn't love me anymore.
* I am sad our relationship is over.
* I will never find anyone like him ever again.

REFRAMING:

Reframing is a Neuro Linguistic Programming (NLP) term. It is a way to view and experience emotions, situations, and/or behaviors in a more positive manner.

At the end of round robin tapping, we can introduce statements to "reframe" the situation.

An example of reframing could be:

* I want this chocolate.
* Maybe eating chocolate is wanting to reconnect to my childhood.
* Maybe eating sugar is a way of being loved.
* Maybe I can find a different way of being loved.

Round robin tapping, scripts, can desensitize the hurt and pain. It can heal the pain of our story. It may not rewrite the beliefs. To clear out the beliefs, it would be necessary to look at the reasons the relationship didn't work and why our heart is broken, or why we crave chocolate.

Round robin/script tapping can also be done by just tapping the side of the hand.

SIDE OF HAND TAPPING TO DESENSITIZE A STORY, SITUATION, AND/OR MEMORY

Just as in the round robin tapping/scripts, we said different statements, one after the other, we can say the same statements and just tap the side of the hand.

If a memory still "haunts" us, embarrasses us, and/or affects our actions in any way, this technique might be perfect to neutralize the memory.

For example:

As Sasha remembers the first dance she attended as a teen-ager, tears well up in her eyes. She starts to tap the side of the hand (SOH) as she tells her story:

My best friend, Samantha and I, were so excited about attending our first high school dance. We weren't old enough to drive so Sam's dad dropped us off in front of the high school auditorium where the dance was held.

(Continue to tap the SOH) We were in awe of how the auditorium was transformed into a palace. Sofas were placed around a hardwood dance floor in the center of the room. We promised each other we would be there for the other throughout the night so neither of us would be stranded alone.

(Continue to tap the SOH) Well, along came Billy McDaniels. Sam had had a crush on Billy since third grade. He asked her to dance and I never saw her again for the rest of the night.

(Continue to tap the SOH) Those three hours were probably the worst night of my entire life! No one asked me to dance. Every time I joined a group of girls, a new song would begin, and every one of them was asked to dance, everyone except me. I don't know why no one asked me to dance. I felt ugly, abandoned, and undesirable! Talk about being a wallflower. I thought I was invisible. I wanted to hide from embarrassment.

(Continue to tap the SOH) This was back in the days before cell phones. The auditorium didn't have a payphone to call my parents to come and get me. I had to endure three hours of humiliation watching every single girl be asked to dance EXCEPT me.

(Continue to tap the SOH) I never attended another high school dance again!

Whether we tap the side of the hand or the eight tapping points, the result is the same. Round robin tapping can desensitize emotions and memories very effectively.

There are different styles of EFT Tapping.
Find the style that works best for your desired result.

Chapter 12
Walking Backwards EFT (Backing Up)

As I was working with a client, they had an issue that was not clearing. Knowing that movement helps to clear issues, I decided to have the person stand up and walk backward. Literally, walk backward, step after step, facing forward while their feet moved backward.

Surprise, surprise, it worked. Every statement cleared as she backed up.

The next client came in. I had him walk backwards, and it worked with clearing issues for him as well. Both clients were somewhat athletic and did workout. I wanted to know if the Backing Up would work with non-athletic people. I was teaching an EFT class the next day. At the end of the class, we all backed up together. And, IT WORKED!

Let's say we want to process, "I will never be comfortable in the world." Stand up. Make sure nothing is behind you. Then walk backward while facing forward and say, "I will never be comfortable in the world. I will never be comfortable in the world. I will never be comfortable in the world. I will never be comfortable in the world." Repeat the phrase six - eight times.

When we back up, we say the same statement we would have made if we were tapping. We don't have to say the "Even though" or the last remainder phrase, "I totally and completely accept myself."

Walking forward represents forward movement in our lives. Walking backward represents the past.

Physical movement can help clear emotional issues and facilitate change.

Walking backward undoes the past and helps to clear, heal, and transform an issue in our lives.

Chapter 13
Intensity Level

One measure of knowing how much an issue has been resolved is to begin, before tapping, by giving the issue an intensity number (IL) between 1 and 10, with 10 being high.

For example, we want a romantic partnership, yet we haven't met "the one." Thinking about a romantic relationship happening, what is the likelihood, on a scale of 1 – 10, with 10 being very likely and 1, not likely at all, of a romantic relationship happening?

Okay. We give ourselves a 2. Now, let's start tapping!

When asked what the issues might be, "Well," we say, "it does not seem as if the people who I want, want me."

Great tapping statement. Tap, "Even though the people I want don't want me, I totally and completely accept myself." After tapping, we check in with ourselves; the IL has gone up to a 4, so it is now a little bit more likely.

What comes to mind now? "No one will find me desirable." Great tapping statement. "Even though no one will find me desirable, I totally and completely accept myself." Check the IL. How likely? 5. Cool! Progress.

What comes to mind now? "I'm not comfortable being vulnerable in romantic relationships." Great tapping statement. "Even though I'm not comfortable being vulnerable in a romantic relationship, I totally and completely accept myself." Check the IL. Now it is a 6. Still progress.

What comes to mind now? "Well, it feels like if I am in a relationship, I will lose a lot of my freedom." Make this into a tapping statement. "Even though I will lose my freedom when I am in a relationship, I totally and completely accept myself." The IL has gone up to a 7.

What comes to mind now? "Oh, if I was in a relationship, I would have to be accountable to someone!" Make this into a tapping statement: "Even though, I would have to be accountable to someone if I was in a relationship, I totally and completely accept myself." Wow...the IL is 9, very likely!

Giving an issue an Intensity Level gives at the beginning and throughout the session gives us an indication of the progress we are making with resolving and/or healing that issue in our lives.

Chapter 14
Yawning and Taking a Deep Breath

From Traditional Chinese Medicine, we know that when chi (energy) flows freely through the meridians, the body is healthy and balanced. Physical, mental, and/or emotional illness can result when the energy is blocked.

Dysfunctional beliefs and emotions produce blocks along the meridians, blocking energy from flowing freely in the body.

With EFT Tapping, as we tap, we release the blocks. As blocked energy is able to flow more freely, the body can now "breathe a sigh of relief." Yawning is that sigh of relief.

If, after tapping, we can take a complete, deep, full, and satisfying breath, we know that an EFT Tapping statement has cleared. This yawn is an indication that an EFT Tapping statement has cleared.

If the yawn or breath is not a full, deep breath then the statement did not clear completely.

Chapter 15
Integration...What Happens After Tapping

After tapping, our system needs some downtime for integration to take place. When the physical body and the mind are "idle," integration can take place.

Sometimes, in the first 24 hours after tapping, we might find ourselves vegging more than normal, sleeping more than normal, or more tired than normal. This downtime is needed to integrate the new changes.

After installing a new program into our computer, sometimes we have to reboot the computer (shut down and restart) for the new program to be integrated into the system.

After tapping, our bodies need to reboot. We need some downtime. When we sleep, the new changes are integrated.

HEALING BEGINS NATURALLY AFTER THE BODY HAS HAD A CHANCE TO INTEGRATE.

Sometimes, after tapping, we forget the intensity of our pain and think that feeling better had nothing to do with tapping. Something so simple could not possibly create the improvement in our state of mind!

When we cut our finger, once it is healed, we don't even remember cutting our finger. As we move toward health, wealth, and well-being, sometimes we don't remember how unhappy, restless, or isolated we once felt.

Chapter 16
EFT Tapping Doesn't Work for Me

Why might EFT Tapping not be working?

* The tapping statement might not be worded such that a dysfunctional belief and/or emotion is addressed and eliminated.
* The style (laser-focused style vs round robin) of tapping may not be effective for the statement to be cleared.
* The EFT Tapping statement is only addressing a symptom and **not the cause of the issue.**

FOR EFT TAPPING TO BE EFFECTIVE, THE CAUSE OF THE ISSUE NEEDS TO BE HEALED.

* Having an awareness of our issues does not heal the dysfunctional beliefs.
* Forgiving ourselves and/or someone else does not heal the dysfunctional beliefs.
* Talk therapy does not heal the dysfunctional beliefs.
* Desensitizing the emotions does not heal the dysfunctional beliefs.
* Healing the experience of a hurtful event does not change the dysfunctional beliefs.

EFT Tapping works best when

1) the statements are worded to eliminate the dysfunctional beliefs,
2) the most effective style of tapping is utilized, and
3) we are healing the cause, not just the symptoms.

Chapter 17
What to Do if an EFT Tapping Statement
Does Not Clear

When a statement might not clear, turn the statement into a question. The statement, "It's not okay for me to be powerful," didn't clear. **Turn the tapping statement into a question:** "Why isn't it okay for me to be powerful?"

The answer might be:

* Powerful people are ruthless and heartless.
* I am afraid of being powerful.
* Being powerful would change me for the worse.
* Power corrupts.
* People would laugh at me if I tried being powerful.
* I would have to give up my fears and anxieties to be powerful.
* I might be called aggressive if I tried being powerful.
* I do not have the abilities, skills, or qualities to be powerful.
* Others would make fun of me if I tried being powerful.
* Powerful people are thoughtless and self-centered.

With these beliefs, it might not be okay or safe to be powerful or even explore the idea of being powerful. The statements above are tapping statements. Tap the answer to the question.

After tapping the answer to the question, revisit the original statement that did not clear. Most likely, it will now be cleared, and you will be able to take a full, deep, and complete breath.

Chapter 18
Science and EFT Tapping Research

EFT has been researched in more than ten countries by more than sixty investigators whose results have been published in more than twenty different peer-reviewed journals. Two leading researchers are Dawson Church, Ph.D. and David Feinstein, Ph.D.

Dr. Dawson Church, a leading expert on energy psychology and an EFT master, has gathered all the research information, and it can be found on this website: www.EFTUniverse.com.

Two Research Studies

1) Harvard Medical School Studies and the Brain's Stress Response

Studies at the Harvard Medical School reveal that stimulating the body's meridian points significantly reduces activity in a part of the brain called the amygdala.

The amygdala can be thought of as the body's alarm system. When the body is experiencing trauma or fear, the amygdala is triggered, and the body is flooded with cortisol, also known as the stress hormone. The stress response sets up an intricate chain reaction.

The studies showed that stimulating or tapping points along the meridians such as EFT Tapping, drastically reduced and/or eliminated the stress response and the resulting chain reaction.

2) Dr. Dawson Church and Cortisol Reduction

Another significant study was conducted by Dr. Dawson Church. He studied the impact an hour's tapping session had on the cortisol levels of eighty-three subjects. He also measured the cortisol levels of people who received traditional talk therapy and those of a third group who received no treatment at all.

On average, for the eighty-three subjects who completed an hour tapping session, cortisol levels were reduced by 24%. Some subjects experienced a 50% reduction in cortisol levels.

The subjects who completed one hour of traditional talk therapy and those who had completed neither session did not experience any significant cortisol reduction.

Chapter 19
Is Lowering the Cortisol Level Enough to Permanently Change Our Lives?

Several things can lower our cortisol (stress hormone) levels including:
* Power posing
* Meditating
* Laughing
* Exercising regularly
* Listening to music
* Getting a massage
* Eliminating caffeine from our diet
* Eating a balanced, nutritious meal and eliminating processed food

Would performing any of the above activities lower our cortisol level enough to permanently change our lives? Only if the activity eliminates the dysfunctional beliefs on a subconscious level.

All of our thoughts, feelings, actions, reactions, choices, and decisions are preceded by a belief. To change our lives, the dysfunctional beliefs must be eliminated.

Power posing, listening to music, or eating a balanced meal will not permanently change our lives. Exercising will help our physical body but will not delete our dysfunctional beliefs. Laughing will bring us into the present so we will not be drawn into our fears or anger, but it will not change our lives. Meditating helps us to center and balance, but will not change our lives on a permanent basis.

To change our lives, we must be able to recognize, acknowledge, and take ownership of that which we want to change then delete the dysfunctional emotions and beliefs that preceded that what we want to change on a subconscious level.

EFT Tapping will delete dysfunctional emotions and beliefs on a subconscious level if we provide the correct "instructions" to our subconscious mind. We must word the tapping statements in the subconscious' language. We must word the tapping statement so the subconscious mind hears what we want to eliminate.

Chapter 20
Tapping Affirmations

* I am healthy and happy.
* Wealth is pouring into my life.
* I radiate love and happiness.
* I have the perfect job for me.
* I am successful in whatever I do.

If we were to tap "I am healthy and happy now" and we are not, most likely, as we are tapping, we might think, "Yeah, right. Sure. I am healthy and happy. My life sucks. I hate my job. I am always broke. There is never enough money..."

The body knows this is not true. We are not healthy and happy now. When we tap, we might have difficulty remembering what we are saying, lose focus and concentration, and/or the mind drifts.

An EFT Tapping statement is most effective **when** it matches our current belief.

The subconscious does not hear the word "No." One way of tapping affirmations and, at the same time, putting in the positives is to put the word "no" into the tapping statements.

* I am **not** healthy and happy. Subconscious hears: I am healthy and happy.
* Wealth is **not** pouring into my life. Subconscious hears: Wealth is pouring into my life.
* I **do not** radiate love and happiness. Subconscious hears: I radiate love and happiness.
* I **do not** have the perfect job for me. Subconscious hears: I have the perfect job for me.
* I am **not** successful in whatever I do. Subconscious hears: I am successful in whatever I do.

If we repeat affirmations over and over and over before we clear the affirmation with EFT Tapping, repeating the affirmation numerous times will have little effect except to create circumstances in our lives so we can be confronted with the beliefs that do not align with the affirmation.

©Tessa Cason, 2022.

Chapter 21
Finishing Touches (Optional)

Some like to finish their tapping with statements that are centering and calming. If this is you, then you might want to try the 16 statements on the next page or make up those that you like. The statements can be said in any order that works for you.

Tapping Location	Statement
Eyebrow	All is well in my life.
Temple	Every day in every way
Under the Eye	I am fulfilled in every way, every day.
Under the Nose	My blessings appears in rich
Under the Lips	I am an excellent steward of wealth and am blessed with great abundance.
Under the Collarbone Knob	I take complete responsibility
Under the Arm	I have all the tools, skills, and
Top back part of the Head	I know I will be able to handle anything
Eyebrow	All my dreams, hopes, wishes, and goals
Temple	Divine love expressing through me,
Under the Eye	I am comfortable with my life changing.
Under the Nose	I am able to create all that I desire.
Under the Lips	I know what needs to be done and
Under the Collarbone Knob	My health is perfect in every way, physically,
Under the Arm	I invite into my subconscious Archangel Raphael to heal all that needs to be forgiven, released, and redeemed. Cleanse me and free me from it now.
Top back part of the Head	The light of God surrounds me. The love of God enfolds me. The power of God protects me. The presence of God watches over and flows through me.

Chapter 22
How to Use This Book

1. The statements are divided into sections. Read through the statements in one section. As you read a statement, notice if you have any reaction to the statement or feel the statement might be true for you. If so, note the number for that statement.

2. Once you have completed reading all the statements in one section, go back and reread the statements you noted and rate them on a scale of 1 – 10, with 10 being a "biggie."

3. List the top statements.

4. From this list, select one and describe how it plays out in your life. It is important to recognize and identify the pattern. What are the consequences of having this belief? Is there a trigger? How does it begin? How does it benefit you? How has it harmed you? There will be a different example listed in each section.

5. Tap the statements. Statements can be combined for scripts...a different statement on each of the different tapping points in one round of tapping.

6. Describe any flashbacks or memories that you might have had as you were tapping out the statements. Describe any ah-has, insights, and/or thoughts you might have had as a result of tapping the statements.

7. After tapping all the statements, review them to determine if you still have a reaction to any of the statements. If you do, you have several options. One, put a "Why" before the statement. Tap out the answer. Secondly, note that this statement may not have cleared and continue on to the next section. Most likely, after additional statements are tapped, statements that may not have cleared, will clear without having to tap the statement again.

8. Allow some downtime for integration and for the body to heal.

9. The number of sections you do at a time will be up to you. Initially, you might want to do one section to determine if you get tired and need to have some downtime after tapping.

10. The day after tapping, again review the statements you tapped to determine if you still have a reaction. If you do, follow the instructions in #7.

1 – 20 EFT Tapping Statements

The biggest seller is cookbooks and the second is diet books - how not to eat what you've just learned how to cook.

Andy Rooney

1. Food is love.

2. I fail every diet.

3. All diets fail me.

4. I am not lovable.

5. I lack self-esteem.

6. I lack self-respect.

7. I don't like myself.

8. I feel empty inside.

9. I eat when I feel sad.

10. I eat when I am hurt.

11. I eat when I am angry.

12. I deflect compliments.

13. I don't honor my body.

14. Food is my only friend.

15. I lack clarity for my life.

16. I eat when I feel lonely.

17. I don't accept my body.

18. I feel lost and hopeless.

19. I am an emotional eater.

20. I am not lovable as I am.

Journaling Pages for Statements 1 – 20

*Dedication, commitment, and effort are needed to accomplish anything worthwhile.
We need to work hard if we want to achieve success, to accomplish anything
worthwhile. Losing weight and taking care of ourselves is no exception.*

Bob Greene

1. From the tapping statements between 1 – 20, list the top seven statements that you thought or felt applied to you:

1.

2.

3.

4.

5.

6.

7.

2. From this list of seven statements, select one and describe how it plays out in your life. Give an example or two. It is important to recognize and identify the pattern. Is there a trigger? How does it begin? How has it benefited you? How has it harmed you? For instance, are you lovable as you are? Or do you have to prove you are lovable by doing something noteworthy?

3. Tap out the top 7 statements.

4. As you were tapping out the statements, did you have any flashback or memories of the past, any additional insights, and/or ah-ha thoughts? If so, write them down. Make note of them.

21 – 40 EFT Tapping Statements

The moment you commit and quit holding back, all sorts of unforeseen incidents, meetings and material assistance will rise up to help you. The simple act of commitment is a powerful magnet for help.

Napoleon Hill

21. My eating is out of control.

22. I feel guilty when I overeat.

23. My focus is always on food.

24. I overeat when I feel lonely.

25. I am sad I fail diet after diet.

26. I am not able to lose weight.

27. I am an expert at self-abuse.

28. My health is not my priority.

29. I hate myself for overeating.

30. Setbacks mean I have failed.

31. I will never be good enough.

32. I cannot imagine myself thin.

33. I use food to soothe my hurt.

34. I will start my diet tomorrow.

35. I use food to soothe my pain.

36. I have lost interest in my life.

37. I am inferior to other people.

38. I don't love or accept myself.

39. I often feel inferior to others.

40. I overeat when I am unhappy.

Journaling Pages for Statements 21 - 40

Your biggest problem or difficulty today has been sent to you
at this moment to teach you something you need to know
to be happier and more successful in the future.

Brian Tracy

1. From the tapping statements between 1 – 20, list the top seven statements that you thought or felt applied to you:

1.

2.

3.

4.

5.

6.

7.

2. From this list of seven statements, select one and describe how it plays out in your life. Give an example or two. It is important to recognize and identify the pattern. Is there a trigger? How does it begin? How has it benefited you? How has it harmed you? For instance, is your eating the only area of your life that is out of control? If not, what is the underlying issue(s)? Stress? Lack of self-confidence? Anger, fear, and/or apathy?

3. Tap out the top 7 statements.

4. As you were tapping out the statements, did you have any flashback or memories of the past, any additional insights, and/or ah-ha thoughts? If so, write them down. Make note of them.

41 – 60 EFT Tapping Statements

A lot of people say they want to get out of pain, and I'm sure that's true, but they aren't willing to make healing a high priority. They aren't willing to look inside to see the source of their pain in order to deal with it.

Lindsay Wagner

41. I am obsessed with food.

42. I eat when I feel anxious.

43. I blow every diet I go on.

44. I am a weight loss failure.

45. I am undeserving of love.

46. Fatness runs in my family.

47. I make poor food choices.

48. I stuff myself until it hurts.

49. I eat when I feel deprived.

50. I am disillusioned with life.

51. My goals are unattainable.

52. Food makes me feel good.

53. I overeat when I am afraid.

54. I am not deserving of love.

55. I overeat when I am bored.

56. I am ordinary in every way.

57. I am broken beyond repair.

58. I am afraid of being judged.

59. I depend on others for love.

60. Who I am is not acceptable.

Journaling Pages for Statements 41 – 60

You are unique and if that is not fulfilled,
then something wonderful has been lost.

Martha Graham

1. From the tapping statements between 1 – 20, list the top seven statements that you thought or felt applied to you:

1.

2.

3.

4.

5.

6.

7.

2. From this list of seven statements, select one and describe how it plays out in your life. Give an example or two. It is important to recognize and identify the pattern. Is there a trigger? How does it begin? How has it benefited you? How has it harmed you? For instance, are your goals attainable? If not, then do you even try? Is this your excuse for not trying? Do you feel empowered to create your goals? Are you willing to work toward your goals? Or are you too insecure to pursue that which you really desire?

3. Tap out the top 7 statements.

4. As you were tapping out the statements, did you have any flashback or memories of the past, any additional insights, and/or ah-ha thoughts? If so, write them down. Make note of them.

61 – 80 EFT Tapping Statements

The commonest form of malnutrition in the western world is obesity.

Mervyn Deitel

61. I stay down when I fall down.

62. I am disgusted with my body.

63. I don't make myself a priority.

64. Eating healthy food is boring.

65. I will fail at weight loss if I try.

66. I overeat when I feel unloved.

67. I have no control over my life.

68. I don't have a plan for my life.

69. I am an expert at self-neglect.

70. I am intimidated by obstacles.

71. I feel ashamed after I overeat.

72. I am not conscious when I eat.

73. I overeat when I feel ordinary.

74. I overeat to fill the void inside.

75. I overeat when I feel rejected.

76. I overeat when I feel less than.

77. I am intimidated by challenges.

78. I have no inner sense of worth.

79. I overeat when I am frustrated.

80. Once I start eating I can't stop.

Journaling Pages for Statements 61 – 80

A diet is the penalty we pay for exceeding the feed limit.

Unknown

1. From the tapping statements between 1 – 20, list the top seven statements that you thought or felt applied to you:

1.

2.

3.

4.

5.

6.

7.

2. From this list of seven statements, select one and describe how it plays out in your life. Give an example or two. It is important to recognize and identify the pattern. Is there a trigger? How does it begin? How has it benefited you? How has it harmed you? For instance, are you disgusted with your body? The body we have is the vessel we have been given to move through life. Your car is the vehicle you move around on the roadways. What condition is your car? Do you trash your car as much as you trash your body? Is it easier to trash your body than to do the work to have the body you want?

3. Tap out the top 7 statements.

4. As you were tapping out the statements, did you have any flashback or memories of the past, any additional insights, and/or ah-ha thoughts? If so, write them down. Make note of them.

81 – 100 EFT Tapping Statements

You cannot make footprints in the sands of time if you are sitting on your butt and who wants to make butt prints in the sand of time?

Bob Moawad

81. Eating healthy food is not filling.

82. I hold grudges and don't forgive.

83. It is impossible for me to be thin.

84. My wounds are too deep to heal.

85. I eat whether I am hungry or not.

86. I have no control over what I eat.

87. I have no control over my eating.

88. I am angry that I emotionally eat.

89. I have no willpower around food.

90. I eat when I have been criticized.

91. I overeat when I am stressed out.

92. My thoughts center around food.

93. I lack the courage to lose weight.

94. Life is one problem after another.

95. I lack the patience to lose weight.

96. I eat when I feel no one loves me.

97. I procrastinate and make excuses.

98. I overeat when I need comforting.

99. Criticism bothers me a great deal.

100. My thoughts center about dieting.

Journaling Pages for Statements 81 - 100

The game of life does not
build character. It reveals it.

Heywood Broun

1. From the tapping statements between 1 - 20, list the top seven statements that you thought or felt applied to you:

1.

2.

3.

4.

5.

6.

7.

2. From this list of seven statements, select one and describe how it plays out in your life. Give an example or two. It is important to recognize and identify the pattern. Is there a trigger? How does it begin? How has it benefited you? How has it harmed you? For instance, is it impossible to be thin? Is thin the goal? One extreme to the other? Is this a pattern in your life... one extreme to the other? What about a healthy balance in the middle? Or it is easier to give up since it is impossible to be thin?

3. Tap out the top 7 statements.

4. As you were tapping out the statements, did you have any flashback or memories of the past, any additional insights, and/or ah-ha thoughts? If so, write them down. Make note of them.

101 – 120 EFT Tapping Statements

*You may have a fresh start any moment you choose. This thing
we call "failure" is not the falling down, but the staying down.*

Mary Pickford

101. I avoid living life to the fullest.

102. I think about food all day long.

103. I focus on how far I have to go.

104. I eat when I feel overwhelmed.

105. I don't have a vision for my life.

106. I don't know what I am craving.

107. I only overeat when I am alone.

108. I am helpless to change my life.

109. My dreams have been crushed.

110. I overeat when I am depressed.

111. I don't know how to start anew.

112. I use food to numb my sadness.

113. I am not accepted for who I am.

114. I live my life with the brakes on.

115. I eat when I feel life is hopeless.

116. I am no fun when I am on a diet.

117. I am sadden by my past choices.

118. I overeat when I feel humiliated.

119. My identity is struggle and diets.

120. I lack the tenacity to lose weight.

Journaling Pages for Statements 101 – 120

Some people change when they see the
light, others when they feel the heat.

Caroline Schoeder

1. From the tapping statements between 1 – 20, list the top seven statements that you thought or felt applied to you:

1.

2.

3.

4.

5.

6.

7.

2. From this list of seven statements, select one and describe how it plays out in your life. Give an example or two. It is important to recognize and identify the pattern. Is there a trigger? How does it begin? How has it benefited you? How has it harmed you? For instance, have your dreams been crushed? What are you doing to create new dreams? Or it is easier to play victim and to feel sorry for yourself? Are you waiting for a guarantee before you begin again?

3. Tap out the top 7 statements.

4. As you were tapping out the statements, did you have any flashback or memories of the past, any additional insights, and/or ah-ha thoughts? If so, write them down. Make note of them.

121 – 140 EFT Tapping Statements

People are like guided missiles. Without a target, they wander aimlessly across the horizons and eventually self-destruct.

Edge Keynote

121. I allow my weight to limit my life.

122. My desires will never be fulfilled.

123. I don't have a strategy for my life.

124. The only activity I enjoy is eating.

125. My identity is that of a fat person.

126. I am only happy when I am eating.

127. I eat when I feel inferior to others.

128. I am too depressed to lose weight.

129. I lack the discipline to lose weight.

130. I am angry that I don't love myself.

131. I use food to soothe my loneliness.

132. Food is a way of rewarding myself.

133. I am embarrassed by compliments.

134. I eat without even tasting my food.

135. I am apathetic about losing weight.

136. I am defective, broken, and flawed.

137. I can't be happy until I lose weight.

138. I am filled with fear and self-doubt.

139. I eat for other reasons than hunger.

140. I eat when others judge me harshly.

Journaling Pages for Statements 121 – 140

People are lonely because they build walls instead of bridges.

J. F. Newton

1. From the tapping statements between 1 – 20, list the top seven statements that you thought or felt applied to you:

1.

2.

3.

4.

5.

6.

7.

2. From this list of seven statements, select one and describe how it plays out in your life. Give an example or two. It is important to recognize and identify the pattern. Is there a trigger? How does it begin? How has it benefited you? How has it harmed you? For instance, are you only happy when you are eating? Wow...what a boring life. Is it easier to think about food than to create a happy and fulfilling life? Are you deserving of a happy and fulfilling life?

3. Tap out the top 7 statements.

4. As you were tapping out the statements, did you have any flashback or memories of the past, any additional insights, and/or ah-ha thoughts? If so, write them down. Make note of them.

141 – 160 EFT Tapping Statements

If you keep doing what you have always done, you
will keep getting what you have always gotten.

Peter Francisco

141. Eating healthy food is not fulfilling.

142. I am angry no one values who I am.

143. I will never be happy with my body.

144. Food is my only source of pleasure.

145. I eat when I feel life is meaningless.

146. I blame my problems on my weight.

147. I lack the motivation to lose weight.

148. I criticize, dislike, and reject myself.

149. I am hurt when someone insults me.

150. I get angry at myself after I overeat.

151. Food is a reward for good behavior.

152. I feel angry and sick when I overeat.

153. My overeating proves I am a failure.

154. I don't celebrate my little successes.

155. I am not important and don't matter.

156. I am not special enough to be loved.

157. I feel ashamed that I am overweight.

158. I continue to eat even after I am full.

159. I lack the self-esteem to lose weight.

160. I expect the worst to always happen.

Journaling Pages for Statements 141 – 160

The difference between a successful person and others is not a
lack of strength, not a lack of knowledge, but rather in a lack of will.

Vince Lombardi

1. From the tapping statements between 1 – 20, list the top seven statements that you thought or felt applied to you:

1.

2.

3.

4.

5.

6.

7.

2. From this list of seven statements, select one and describe how it plays out in your life. Give an example or two. It is important to recognize and identify the pattern. Is there a trigger? How does it begin? How has it benefited you? How has it harmed you? For instance, are you filled with fear and self-doubt? Is this your excuse for not learning new skills? Is it easier to be a coward than to apply yourself learning new skills?

3. Tap out the top 7 statements.

4. As you were tapping out the statements, did you have any flashback or memories of the past, any additional insights, and/or ah-ha thoughts? If so, write them down. Make note of them.

161 – 180 EFT Tapping Statements

*Always bear in mind that your own resolution to succeed is
more important than any other one thing.*

Abraham Lincoln

161. I don't love, honor, or cherish myself.

162. I lack the courage to live my life fully.

163. I lack the commitment to lose weight.

164. I am afraid to be visible and beautiful.

165. I have given up on myself and my life.

166. Food is the only way I nurture myself.

167. Food is a way of showing myself love.

168. My emotional wounds will never heal.

169. I use food to stuff down my emotions.

170. My fatness confirms my lack of worth.

171. I will never be able to lose the weight.

172. I sabotage my own weight loss efforts.

173. I lack the focus needed to lose weight.

174. It is doubtful I can turn my life around.

175. I can't handle another disappointment.

176. It is too much work to lose this weight.

177. My happiness does not depend on me.

178. I don't eat foods that nourish my body.

179. I don't exercise enough to lose weight.

180. I continue to indulge after I messed up.

Journaling Pages for Statements 161 – 180

*As difficult as it seems, you can be sure of this: At the core of the heart, you have
the power to move beyond the old issues that are still hindering your freedom.
The hardest things—the ones that push you up against your limits—are the
very things you need to address to make a quantum leap into a fresh inner and outer life.*

Doc Childre and Howard Martin

1. From the tapping statements between 1 – 20, list the top seven statements that you thought or felt applied to you:

1.

2.

3.

4.

5.

6.

7.

2. From this list of seven statements, select one and describe how it plays out in your life. Give an example or two. It is important to recognize and identify the pattern. Is there a trigger? How does it begin? How has it benefited you? How has it harmed you? For instance, is it impossible to eat healthy? Is it the taste of healthy food you don't like? Is it the time to prepare healthy foods? What is it about eating healthy that is difficult? Or is that the excuse so you can continue to indulge in fast food and foods you crave?

3. Tap out the top 7 statements.

4. As you were tapping out the statements, did you have any flashback or memories of the past, any additional insights, and/or ah-ha thoughts? If so, write them down. Make note of them.

181 – 200 EFT Tapping Statements

*A kite flies best when the wind blows in one
direction and the string pulls from another.*

Henry Ford

181. I am angry at, and punishing, myself.

182. I lack the self-control to lose weight.

183. I give up too easily on losing weight.

184. My cravings are in control of my life.

185. I judge others and/or myself harshly.

186. I am sad that I am invisible to others.

187. Food is the one thing I can count on.

188. I am full of self-doubt and insecurity.

189. It is impossible for me to eat healthy.

190. I will never succeed at losing weight.

191. I am afraid to weigh my ideal weight.

192. I overeat when happiness eludes me.

193. I am angry that I sabotage my health.

194. I eat when everything feels hopeless.

195. It is impossible for me to lose weight.

196. I am unaware of when and what I eat.

197. I make excuses for being overweight.

198. Food is the solution when I am upset.

199. I overeat even when I am not hungry.

200. I feel defeated, beaten, and bankrupt.

Journaling Pages for Statements 181 – 200

*The wonderful thing about the game of life is that
winning and losing are only temporary...unless you quit.*

Fred Mills

1. From the tapping statements between 1 – 20, list the top seven statements that you thought or felt applied to you:

1.

2.

3.

4.

5.

6.

7.

2. From this list of seven statements, select one and describe how it plays out in your life. Give an example or two. It is important to recognize and identify the pattern. Is there a trigger? How does it begin? How has it benefited you? How has it harmed you? For instance, do you lack the courage to live your life fully? Is it about courage or you don't know what would fulfill you? Is it easier to eat than to explore life and your life?

3. Tap out the top 7 statements.

4. As you were tapping out the statements, did you have any flashback or memories of the past, any additional insights, and/or ah-ha thoughts? If so, write them down. Make note of them.

201 – 220 EFT Tapping Statements

Opportunity may knock only once.
Temptation leans on the doorbell.

Unknown

201. I don't know what is missing in my life.

202. I eat when I am overwhelmed with life.

203. I am angry that I yo-yo with my weight.

204. I reward myself with my favorite foods.

205. I am not empowered to change my life.

206. I give up when obstacles block my way.

207. My thinking is not positive or powerful.

208. I have no idea how to eat to be healthy.

209. I don't know how to deal with setbacks.

210. I am powerless to create the life I want.

211. I don't know how to create what I want.

212. I've given up on my dreams and myself.

213. I can't resist the foods I crave the most.

214. I am destined to be overweight forever.

215. It is difficult to make it through the day.

216. I am not committed to being successful.

217. I use my excess weight to keep me safe.

218. I don't have the patience to lose weight.

219. Others see as me as flawed and inferior.

220. I hate that others stare at me when I eat.

Journaling Pages for Statements 201 – 220

*Let us not look back in anger or forward
in fear, but around in awareness.*

James Thurber

1. From the tapping statements between 1 – 20, list the top seven statements that you thought or felt applied to you:

1.

2.

3.

4.

5.

6.

7.

2. From this list of seven statements, select one and describe how it plays out in your life. Give an example or two. It is important to recognize and identify the pattern. Is there a trigger? How does it begin? How has it benefited you? How has it harmed you? For instance, do you reward yourself with your favorite foods? Is this to make you feel better or worse? Is this a way to punish yourself or reward yourself? Is this a way to sabotage yourself or make you feel better?

3. Tap out the top 7 statements.

4. As you were tapping out the statements, did you have any flashback or memories of the past, any additional insights, and/or ah-ha thoughts? If so, write them down. Make note of them.

221 – 240 EFT Tapping Statements

In the long run, we shape our lives and we shape ourselves.
The process never ends until we die.
And the choices we make are ultimately our responsibility.

Eleanor Roosevelt

221. Losing weight will always be a struggle.

222. I am totally hopeless and full of despair.

223. I feel alone, invisible, and disconnected.

224. I cannot accept compliments graciously.

225. Eating is not a conscious activity for me.

226. I don't know how to heal what is broken.

227. I am constantly finding fault with myself.

228. I feel inadequate, unworthy, and inferior.

229. I can't lose weight because of my genes.

230. I overeat when others find fault with me.

231. I feel huge and fat when I look at myself.

232. Food is available when I feel abandoned.

233. I don't feel deserving, worthy, or lovable.

234. I don't know how to overcome obstacles.

235. I am angry at other people's insensitivity.

236. I am not conscious of what or when I eat.

237. I am sad that diet after diet has failed me.

238. I cannot successfully get past temptation.

239. I don't have the energy to change my life.

240. It is too hard to stop the emotional eating.

Journaling Pages for Statements 221 – 240

Our suffering comes from wanting things to be different.
When we stop that, our suffering stops.
We can want things. It is the needing that must stop.

Wayne Dyer

1. From the tapping statements between 1 – 20, list the top seven statements that you thought or felt applied to you:

1.

2.

3.

4.

5.

6.

7.

2. From this list of seven statements, select one and describe how it plays out in your life. Give an example or two. It is important to recognize and identify the pattern. Is there a trigger? How does it begin? How has it benefited you? How has it harmed you? For instance, is your adequacy based on your success with weight loss? Is this about self-worth, confidence, learning new skills, and/or working toward a goal? Or that you lack the tools and skills to be successful and aren't doing anything to develop the tools and skills to be successful?

3. Tap out the top 7 statements.

4. As you were tapping out the statements, did you have any flashback or memories of the past, any additional insights, and/or ah-ha thoughts? If so, write them down. Make note of them.

241 – 260 EFT Tapping Statements

*Good health is more than just exercise and diet. It's really a
point of view and a mental attitude you have about yourself.*

Angela Lansbury

241. I don't know what loving myself looks like.

242. I don't know how to heal my hurt and pain.

243. I stuff my feelings instead of healing them.

244. I cannot imagine myself at my ideal weight.

245. I am sad that my weight has limited my life.

246. Eating is the only pleasure I have in my life.

247. My food choices are made by my emotions.

248. I don't have conscious control of my habits.

249. I wait to do anything until I lose the weight.

250. I will never lose weight if I accept my body.

251. I am angry that I depend on others for love.

252. I don't know how to lose the excess weight.

253. My daily workout is not sacred or a priority.

254. The only image I have of myself is being fat.

255. My identity is that of an overweight person.

256. I overeat when I feel I am not good enough.

257. I am angry that I sabotage myself with food.

258. I am afraid to be happy, healthy, and strong.

259. It is impossible for me to succeed at dieting.

260. I overeat when I don't want to feel anything.

Journaling Pages for Statements 241 - 260

Having experienced, struggled with, and come to terms with my own particular share of 'necessary losses' over the years, I've come to realize that those losses have taught me some of life's most valuable lessons.

Marty Tousley

1. From the tapping statements between 1 – 20, list the top seven statements that you thought or felt applied to you:

1.

2.

3.

4.

5.

6.

7.

2. From this list of seven statements, select one and describe how it plays out in your life. Give an example or two. It is important to recognize and identify the pattern. Is there a trigger? How does it begin? How has it benefited you? How has it harmed you? For instance, do you stuff your feelings instead of healing them? Do you stuff yourself until you are beyond full? What would happen if you felt your feelings? Would you be overwhelmed if you felt your feelings?

3. Tap out the top 7 statements.

4. As you were tapping out the statements, did you have any flashback or memories of the past, any additional insights, and/or ah-ha thoughts? If so, write them down. Make note of them.

261 – 280 EFT Tapping Statements

Sometimes life pushes us and there is
usually wisdom in it that we only see later.

Diane Gilman

261. I don't know who I would be if I was thin.

262. It is impossible for me to lose this weight.

263. I use my weight to avoid moving forward.

264. I eat when I don't feel I belong anywhere.

265. I lack the tools and skills to be successful.

266. I use food to satisfy my emotional hunger.

267. I will never be able to look the way I want.

268. I don't know how to overcome difficulties.

269. I don't learn valuable lessons from defeat.

270. I lack the desire to lose the excess weight.

271. I am angry at myself for being overweight.

272. I am not comfortable around other people.

273. I feel depressed and guilty when I overeat.

274. I am powerless to stop gorging when I eat.

275. I continue to indulge all day once I blow it.

276. My self-talk is more negative than positive.

277. I am angry that I need others to feel loved.

278. I lack the mental toughness to lose weight.

279. I don't have the courage to change my life.

280. Joy comes after successfully losing weight.

Journaling Pages for Statements 261 – 280

We all fall into patterns and ruts.
It takes courage, confidence, and
guts to jump out of the ruts.

· *Unknown*

1. From the tapping statements between 1 – 20, list the top seven statements that you thought or felt applied to you:

1.

2.

3.

4.

5.

6.

7.

2. From this list of seven statements, select one and describe how it plays out in your life. Give an example or two. It is important to recognize and identify the pattern. Is there a trigger? How does it begin? How has it benefited you? How has it harmed you? For instance, do you use your weight to avoid moving forward? If it wasn't weight, would it be something else? Is it easier to stagnate than have goals and commit to the goals? Does the thought of moving forward feel like stepping into a dark forest without a flashlight?

3. Tap out the top 7 statements.

4. As you were tapping out the statements, did you have any flashback or memories of the past, any additional insights, and/or ah-ha thoughts? If so, write them down. Make note of them.

281 – 300 EFT Tapping Statements

Less than and not good enough destroy hope and keep us lost in maze called "survival."
The only way out of survival is to heal the feeling of not being good enough.
The only way to change not being good enough is to heal the underlying beliefs.

Tessa Cason

281. I know I will fail at weight loss before I begin.

282. Eating is the only enjoyment I have in my life.

283. I don't know who I would be without my pain.

284. Releasing resentment will not dissolve my fat.

285. I am super-sensitive to criticism and rejection.

286. Disappointment leads to my emotional eating.

287. I will never be able to sustain my ideal weight.

288. My behavior is not consistent with my desires.

289. I allow others to sabotage my weight program.

290. I lack the self-confidence weight loss requires.

291. I am not consistent in my weight loss program.

292. I eat out of habit and not because I am hungry.

293. I am angry that I gain weight just by breathing.

294. Trying to lose weight puts me into overwhelm.

295. I don't know how to stop the emotional eating.

296. Not being loved leads to my being overweight.

297. I resent others telling me how and what to eat.

298. I am tired of wearing clothes to hide my shape.

299. Being overweight proves I am less than others.

300. I overeat to cover up feelings I cannot express.

Journaling Pages for Statements 281 – 300

Over time, unhealed grief becomes anger, blame, resentment, righteousness, and/or remorse. We become someone we are not. It takes courage to move through the grief and all the emotions buried deep within. The depth of our pain is an indication the importance and significance something has for us.

Tessa Cason

1. From the tapping statements between 1 – 20, list the top seven statements that you thought or felt applied to you:

1.

2.

3.

4.

5.

6.

7.

2. From this list of seven statements, select one and describe how it plays out in your life. Give an example or two. It is important to recognize and identify the pattern. Is there a trigger? How does it begin? How has it benefited you? How has it harmed you? For instance, is your behavior consistent with your desires? Congruency...actions match your words...walk your talk. Do you speak before you think? Is it easier to say what you will do rather than to do what you say you will do? To know someone's intent...listen to their actions.

3. Tap out the top 7 statements.

4. As you were tapping out the statements, did you have any flashback or memories of the past, any additional insights, and/or ah-ha thoughts? If so, write them down. Make note of them.

301 - 320 EFT Tapping Statements

Courage is doing what you're afraid to do.
There can be no courage unless you're scared.

Eddie Rickenbacker

301. I am not willing to give up my comfort food.

302. It is hopeless that anything will work for me.

303. I have missed out so much on life and living.

304. I am angry that I can't eat like everyone else.

305. I am not capable of losing the excess weight.

306. I don't know how to overcome loss or defeat.

307. I'm tired of dieting and always having to diet.

308. I don't stop eating when I am satisfied or full.

309. I am overwhelmed with a sense of emptiness.

310. I am not in charge of my life or my behaviors.

311. I will never be able to lose the excess weight.

312. I eat without thinking about what I am eating.

313. I can't lose weight because of my upbringing.

314. I can't lose weight because of my personality.

315. Being stressed leads to my being overweight.

316. I always eat the food offered to me by others.

317. Being rejected leads to my being overweight.

318. I am not committed to a total health program.

319. Nothing good is ever going to happen for me.

320. I am angry that to be healthy I have to be thin.

Journaling Pages for Statements 301 - 320

*Don't wait for your ship to
come in. Row out to meet it.*

Unknown

1. From the tapping statements between 1 – 20, list the top seven statements that you thought or felt applied to you:

1.

2.

3.

4.

5.

6.

7.

2. From this list of seven statements, select one and describe how it plays out in your life. Give an example or two. It is important to recognize and identify the pattern. Is there a trigger? How does it begin? How has it benefited you? How has it harmed you? For instance, are you not in charge of my life? If not, do you play the blame game? "It's their fault I can't have what I want!" When you blame and are not in charge of your life, you don't take ownership of your life. Is it easier to be the victim or victor?

3. Tap out the top 7 statements.

4. As you were tapping out the statements, did you have any flashback or memories of the past, any additional insights, and/or ah-ha thoughts? If so, write them down. Make note of them.

321 – 340 EFT Tapping Statements

*Every adversity, every failure, every heartache carries
with it the seed of an equal or greater benefit.*

Napoleon Hill

321. Eating healthy food is emotionally unsatisfying.

322. Not liking myself leads to my being overweight.

323. I overeat when my needs are not being fulfilled.

324. I am not committed to losing the excess weight.

325. I eat when I feel rejected, unloved, and isolated.

326. I am angry I am holding onto this excess weight.

327. I lack the motivation to successfully lose weight.

328. I overeat due to problems and turmoil in my life.

329. After losing weight, I regain all the weight I lost.

330. The stress to lose weight makes me gain weight.

331. I am overwhelmed with a sense of hopelessness.

332. I am not able to concentrate on long-term goals.

333. The lack of peace leads to my being overweight.

334. Feeling worthless leads to my being overweight.

335. I hate that others judge me based on my weight.

336. I am not willing to put forth extraordinary effort.

337. Not being wanted leads to my being overweight.

338. I overeat when I am anticipating disappointment.

339. I am not consistent in pursuing a health program.

340. I fear rejection and not being accepted by others.

Journaling Pages for Statements 321 - 340

When we set exciting worthwhile goals for ourselves, they
work in two ways. We work on them and they work on us.

Bob Moawad

1. From the tapping statements between 1 – 20, list the top seven statements that you thought or felt applied to you:

1.

2.

3.

4.

5.

6.

7.

2. From this list of seven statements, select one and describe how it plays out in your life. Give an example or two. It is important to recognize and identify the pattern. Is there a trigger? How does it begin? How has it benefited you? How has it harmed you? For instance, will you regain back the weight you lose after losing it? 95% of people that do lose weight put the weight back on. The odds are in favor of gaining it back...UNLESS, you change the dysfunctional, mis-beliefs on a subconscious level. Healing the beliefs change the thoughts, feelings, actions, reactions, choices, and decisions we make about food.

3. Tap out the top 7 statements.

4. As you were tapping out the statements, did you have any flashback or memories of the past, any additional insights, and/or ah-ha thoughts? If so, write them down. Make note of them.

341 - 360 EFT Tapping Statements

*Our greatest weakness lies in giving up. The most
certain way to succeed is always to try just one more time.*

Thomas Edison

341. The only control I have in my life is what I eat.

342. Life is synonymous with survival and hardship.

343. I don't know who I am without my food issues.

344. My goals are not within my realm of capability.

345. I berate myself for my real and imagined flaws.

346. I haven't taken responsibility for my health yet.

347. Being frustrated leads to my being overweight.

348. I live my life in constant regret and depression.

349. I don't know how to deal with disappointments.

350. I am a victim when it comes to food and eating.

351. The only way to lose weight is to starve myself.

352. I eat when I want to avoid feeling my emotions.

353. I lack the determination to keep on keeping on.

354. I ignore the voice that tells me I am overeating.

355. Meals are anxious and unpleasant times for me.

356. I am angry that to be healthy I have to exercise.

357. Healthy food is like eating cardboard and grass.

358. Feeling hopeless leads to my being overweight.

359. I cannot overcome my defects and deficiencies.

360. I am afraid of being abandoned and/or rejected.

Journaling Pages for Statements 341 - 360

Anger on David Hawkins' Map of Consciousness calibrates at 150.
Courage is 200. It does not take courage to get angry.
It does take courage to climb up to courage to heal the anger.

Tessa Cason

1. From the tapping statements between 1 – 20, list the top seven statements that you thought or felt applied to you:

1.

2.

3.

4.

5.

6.

7.

2. From this list of seven statements, select one and describe how it plays out in your life. Give an example or two. It is important to recognize and identify the pattern. Is there a trigger? How does it begin? How has it benefited you? How has it harmed you? For instance, does frustration lead to your being overweight? Frustration is anger. Is it easier to be frustrated than to heal the anger?

3. Tap out the top 7 statements.

4. As you were tapping out the statements, did you have any flashback or memories of the past, any additional insights, and/or ah-ha thoughts? If so, write them down. Make note of them.

361 – 380 EFT Tapping Statements

Hope is a higher heart frequency, and as you begin to re-connect with your heart, hope is waiting to show you new possibilities and arrest the downward spiral of grief and loneliness. Listening to the still small voice in your heart will make hope into a reality.

Sara Paddison

361. My life would be different if I could lose weight.

362. I don't have the skills or tools to lose this weight.

363. I am not willing to do what I must to lose weight.

364. I won't be able to relate to others if I lost weight.

365. I overeat in an attempt to fulfill my unmet needs.

366. Feeling powerless leads to my being overweight.

367. I would have to examine my life to be successful.

368. Food fills me up when I feel empty and depleted.

369. My food choices are not consistent with my goal.

370. I lack the persistence to successfully lose weight.

371. I am not deserving of good health and happiness.

372. I give into my food cravings when I feel less than.

373. I have a constant sense of emptiness and despair.

374. I overeat to comfort myself in stressful situations.

375. I sabotage my health program to remain invisible.

376. I fall short every time I compare myself to others.

377. I get angry if anyone comments about my weight.

378. I stay heavy so that others feel secure around me.

379. I lack the inner strength necessary to lose weight.

380. I am tired of the stares I get for being overweight.

Journaling Pages for Statements 361 - 380

*Being overweight helps many fearful people feel as if they
are invisible. They seek ways to sabotage themselves in order
to return to the safety that their excess weight provides.*

Bob Greene

1. From the tapping statements between 1 – 20, list the top seven statements that you thought or felt applied to you:

1.

2.

3.

4.

5.

6.

7.

2. From this list of seven statements, select one and describe how it plays out in your life. Give an example or two. It is important to recognize and identify the pattern. Is there a trigger? How does it begin? How has it benefited you? How has it harmed you? For instance, do you sabotage your weight loss program? Would you be able to maintain your ideal weight once you lost the excess weight? Do you sabotage other areas of your life?

3. Tap out the top 7 statements.

4. As you were tapping out the statements, did you have any flashback or memories of the past, any additional insights, and/or ah-ha thoughts? If so, write them down. Make note of them.

381 – 400 EFT Tapping Statements

The road to success has many tempting parking places.

Steve Potter

381. Food is the one thing I allow myself to indulge in.

382. I will not feel happy until I weigh my ideal weight.

383. I can't imagine my life without my food problems.

384. I can't lose weight because of my body chemistry.

385. My weight is an impossible obstacle to overcome.

386. I am angry that I will never be able to lose weight.

387. I don't have a clear vision of my weight loss goals.

388. I use food to change my focus away from my pain.

389. Losing weight pushes me out of my comfort zone.

390. I am unwilling to make the time to exercise/move.

391. I don't know how to re-chart my path after defeat.

392. I don't have the tools to deal with disappointment.

393. Overeating is synonymous with happiness and joy.

394. I have failed every time I have tried to lose weight.

395. I am not willing to ask for support/help/assistance.

396. I constantly beat myself up about my food choices.

397. It is impossible for me to succeed at losing weight.

398. I don't have the courage to weigh my ideal weight.

399. Not being accepted leads to my being overweight.

400. Eating gives me something to do when I am bored.

Journaling Pages for Statements 381 – 400

*Even a happy life cannot be without a measure of darkness and the word
happiness would lose its meaning if it were not balanced by sadness.*

Carl Jung

1. From the tapping statements between 1 – 20, list the top seven statements that you thought or felt applied to you:

1.

2.

3.

4.

5.

6.

7.

2. From this list of seven statements, select one and describe how it plays out in your life. Give an example or two. It is important to recognize and identify the pattern. Is there a trigger? How does it begin? How has it benefited you? How has it harmed you? For instance, do you lack the persistence to successfully lose weight? Do you lack persistence in other areas of your life or just in trying to lose weight? If in all areas of your life, do you have anything to work toward? Or is it easier to settle for the status quo?

3. Tap out the top 7 statements.

4. As you were tapping out the statements, did you have any flashback or memories of the past, any additional insights, and/or ah-ha thoughts? If so, write them down. Make note of them.

401 – 420 EFT Tapping Statements

Failure is the opportunity to begin again more intelligently.

Henry Ford

401. I will not feel fulfilled until I weigh my ideal weight.

402. I don't expect that I will ever weigh my ideal weight.

403. I hold onto excess weight to numb myself from hurt.

404. The quality of my life is limited by my excess weight.

405. I don't accept myself unconditionally exactly as I am.

406. I am not able to transform my relationship with food.

407. I don't have the will to follow any plan to lose weight.

408. I punish myself after I have eaten more than I should.

409. I don't want others to know how much I weigh or eat.

410. I am angry that I use food as a reward if I lose weight.

411. I am always stressing about what and how much I eat.

412. Food is my only source of comfort, love, and security.

413. I don't have the determination to overcome setbacks.

414. I am not motivated enough to lose the excess weight.

415. I overeat to compensate for what is missing in my life.

416. Not feeling worthwhile leads to my being overweight.

417. Food is always there when there is no one to hold me.

418. Others see me as defective, flawed, and incompetent.

419. Being used and abused leads to my being overweight.

420. I become unraveled when someone judges me harshly.

Journaling Pages for Statements 401 – 420

Anger is our emotional response, our button being
pushed, our issue, and thus, our responsibility to heal.

Tessa Cason

1. From the tapping statements between 1 – 20, list the top seven statements that you thought or felt applied to you:

1.

2.

3.

4.

5.

6.

7.

2. From this list of seven statements, select one and describe how it plays out in your life. Give an example or two. It is important to recognize and identify the pattern. Is there a trigger? How does it begin? How has it benefited you? How has it harmed you? For instance, are you angry that you are ignored because of your weight? Who are you angry at and for what? Are you angry at someone else's judgement of you? Are you angry at yourself that you have given them a reason to judge you? Or is it anger at yourself for putting you in a vulnerable position in which you are judged by your outer appearance?

3. Tap out the top 7 statements.

4. As you were tapping out the statements, did you have any flashback or memories of the past, any additional insights, and/or ah-ha thoughts? If so, write them down. Make note of them.

421 – 440 EFT Tapping Statements

There are no secrets to success. It is the result of preparation, hard work, and learning from failure.

Colin Powell

421. I am having difficulty finding meaning in anything.

422. It's impossible to love myself with the body I have.

423. I am not willing to move beyond the ache for food.

424. My health and well-being are not my top priorities.

425. I don't take small steps every day toward my goals.

426. I am angry that I am ignored because of my weight.

427. I have given up hope that my life will ever improve.

428. My identity is tied up in my struggle to lose weight.

429. It is hopeless that I will ever weigh my ideal weight.

430. I will regain back all the weight I lose after losing it.

431. I have tried and failed so many times to lose weight.

432. I am not committed to permanent lifestyle changes.

433. I don't have what it takes to succeed at weight loss.

434. I lack the determination to successfully lose weight.

435. I will never be able to move beyond my food issues.

436. Food fills the emptiness of not having anyone close.

437. I reach for food when I want and need to feel loved.

438. I am sad that others only see my weight and not me.

439. I am not totally committed to a weight loss program.

440. I eat smaller portions when other people are around.

Journaling Pages for Statements 421 – 440

When we hold someone responsible for what we experience, we lose power.
When we depend upon another person for the experiences we think are necessary
to our well-being, we live continually in the fear that they will not deliver.

Gary Zukav

1. From the tapping statements between 1 – 20, list the top seven statements that you thought or felt applied to you:

1.

2.

3.

4.

5.

6.

7.

2. From this list of seven statements, select one and describe how it plays out in your life. Give an example or two. It is important to recognize and identify the pattern. Is there a trigger? How does it begin? How has it benefited you? How has it harmed you? For instance, do you use food to feel loved? Does food = love? Is it easier to relate to food? Do you know how to relate to people? Is there a fear of possibly being rejected if you tried to connect with someone? Little chance of being rejected by food.

3. Tap out the top 7 statements.

4. As you were tapping out the statements, did you have any flashback or memories of the past, any additional insights, and/or ah-ha thoughts? If so, write them down. Make note of them.

441 – 460 EFT Tapping Statements

*Hiding in my room, safe within my womb, I touch no one and no one touches me.
I am a rock, I am an island. And a rock feels no pain and an island never cries.*

Paul Simon from song I Am a Rock

441. I don't know what size portion of foods would fill me up.

442. I am not sure I would know who I am without the weight.

443. I would rather be invisible than to weigh my ideal weight.

444. I don't know who I would be if I weighed my ideal weight.

445. I overeat to mask my feelings of sadness, fear, and anger.

446. I am not willing to give up food as my coping mechanism.

447. Food is always there when there is no one to comfort me.

448. Obsessing about food is a distraction from my real issues.

449. I am doing everything right and still can't lose the weight.

450. Overeating is synonymous with reward and job well done.

451. I don't have the perseverance that losing weight requires.

452. I am always thinking about and struggling with my weight.

453. I overeat when I am craving affection and companionship.

454. Overeating is synonymous with shame and worthlessness.

455. To maintain my ideal weight, I have to eat less than a bird.

456. I would have to constantly diet for permanent weight loss.

457. I will never be able to permanently weigh my ideal weight.

458. I feel ashamed/guilty that I cannot lose weight on my own.

459. I would have to take ownership of my life to be successful.

460. This excess weight has prevented me from so many things.

Journaling Pages for Statements 441 - 460

Brain cells come and brain cells go, but fat cells live forever.

Unknown

1. From the tapping statements between 1 – 20, list the top seven statements that you thought or felt applied to you:

1.

2.

3.

4.

5.

6.

7.

2. From this list of seven statements, select one and describe how it plays out in your life. Give an example or two. It is important to recognize and identify the pattern. Is there a trigger? How does it begin? How has it benefited you? How has it harmed you? For instance, would you rather be invisible than to weigh your ideal weight? What is your fear about being visible? Attention? Career advancement? New friendships and/or relationships? With any of these, your life would change. Would you rather your life stay the same?

3. Tap out the top 7 statements.

4. As you were tapping out the statements, did you have any flashback or memories of the past, any additional insights, and/or ah-ha thoughts? If so, write them down. Make note of them.

461 – 480 EFT Tapping Statements

Anger is about the past. Fear is about the future.
Fear may actually be anger that we will fail again in the future.

Tessa Cason

461. I overeat when I don't know how to handle a situation.

462. I cannot picture myself reaching my goal/ideal weight.

463. Thinking about losing weight puts me into overwhelm.

464. I am not able to fill my emotional emptiness by myself.

465. The only way I know how to handle loneliness is to eat.

466. I have failed at every attempt to heal my weight issues.

467. I am not willing to give up my favorite unhealthy foods.

468. I don't have the mental toughness weight loss requires.

469. I overeat when I am stressed, afraid, and overwhelmed.

470. No matter what I do, I will never be able to lose weight.

471. I am intimidated by the possibility of others judging me.

472. Feeling stupid and dumb leads to my being overweight.

473. The only way I know how to handle overwhelm is to eat.

474. I blame others for my inability to reach my weight goals.

475. I avoid _____ because of my weight.

476. No one asks me to lunch when they know I am on a diet.

477. Anxiety and being worried lead to my being overweight.

478. I don't have short-term realistic goals to lose the weight.

479. I am sad that others can't see pass the weight to see me.

480. Healthy food choices are not a natural way of life for me.

Journaling Pages for Statements 461 – 480

Those on top of the mountain did not fall there.

Marcus Washling

1. From the tapping statements between 1 – 20, list the top seven statements that you thought or felt applied to you:

1.

2.

3.

4.

5.

6.

7.

2. From this list of seven statements, select one and describe how it plays out in your life. Give an example or two. It is important to recognize and identify the pattern. Is there a trigger? How does it begin? How has it benefited you? How has it harmed you? For instance, you cannot picture yourself reaching your goal/ideal weight. Is this because you don't want to be disappointed if you don't reach your goal? Do you think you would be setting yourself up for embarrassment if you did picture yourself at your ideal weight and then didn't reach your goal?

3. Tap out the top 7 statements.

4. As you were tapping out the statements, did you have any flashback or memories of the past, any additional insights, and/or ah-ha thoughts? If so, write them down. Make note of them.

481 – 500 EFT Tapping Statements

Every human being is the author of his own health or disease.

Buddha

481. I bribe myself with ___ to force myself to do a "should."

482. I have an addictive personality...overeating, overworking...

483. Difficulty in my relationships lead to my being overweight.

484. I feel life would be a lot different if I could lose this weight.

485. I lack the patience necessary to improve my life and health.

486. Too much conflicting information to be able to lose weight.

487. The only way I know how to handle the depression is to eat.

488. Those around me sabotage my health/weight loss program.

489. I am angry that I eat well and the weight does not come off.

490. The solution to permanent weight lose is impossible for me.

491. I am sad that I don't have the courage to pursue my dreams.

492. I lack the inner strength needed to successfully lose weight.

493. I am under too much stress to successful work on my health.

494. I lack the motivation to continue when the going gets rough.

495. I am sad that I have not been successful at losing the weight.

496. I overeat when someone makes a comment about my weight.

497. It takes too much energy and effort to reach my ideal weight.

498. It is hopeless that I will ever be able to lose the excess weight.

499. Something always sabotages my commitment to losing weight.

500. It makes me really uncomfortable to eat in front of thin people.

Journaling Pages for Statements 481 - 500

Men and women are limited not by the place of their birth,
not by the color of their skin, but by the size of their hope.

John Johnson

1. From the tapping statements between 1 – 20, list the top seven statements that you thought or felt applied to you:

1.

2.

3.

4.

5.

6.

7.

2. From this list of seven statements, select one and describe how it plays out in your life. Give an example or two. It is important to recognize and identify the pattern. Is there a trigger? How does it begin? How has it benefited you? How has it harmed you? For instance, does something always sabotages your commitment to losing weight? Is it easier to be fail than to succeed?

3. Tap out the top 7 statements.

4. As you were tapping out the statements, did you have any flashback or memories of the past, any additional insights, and/or ah-ha thoughts? If so, write them down. Make note of them.

501 – 520 EFT Tapping Statements

Don't measure yourself by what you've accomplished,
but rather by what you should have accomplished with your abilities.

John Wooden

501. I lack the discipline necessary to improve my life and health.

502. I cannot see myself completing and accomplishing my goals.

503. I don't have the patience to stick to my weight loss program.

504. Not being in control of my life leads to my being overweight.

505. I don't know which plan is the best plan for me to lose weight.

506. I am angry that others don't support my effects to lose weight.

507. I am angry that all the dieting I do only to gain back the weight.

508. I am not committed to reaching or maintaining my ideal weight.

509. I am sad that my life has been diminished by the excess weight.

510. I am overwhelmed with the amount of fat/weight I have to lose.

511. I don't have the persistence to stick to my weight loss program.

512. Overeating is synonymous with love and emotional satisfaction.

513. I don't have the courage to make permanent changes in my life.

514. I don't have the energy to explore buried feelings about my life.

515. Problems are overwhelming obstacles I am unable to overcome.

516. I am angry that others judge me based on my outer appearance.

517. I don't have the self-control to maintain my weight loss program.

518. My only identity is that of a fat person, struggling to lose weight.

519. I am angry that I take care of my health and I am still overweight.

520. I deprive my body of the nourishing foods it needs to sustain life.

Journaling Pages for Statements 501 - 520

No man can think clearly when his fists are clenched.

George Jean Nathan

1. From the tapping statements between 1 – 20, list the top seven statements that you thought or felt applied to you:

1.

2.

3.

4.

5.

6.

7.

2. From this list of seven statements, select one and describe how it plays out in your life. Give an example or two. It is important to recognize and identify the pattern. Is there a trigger? How does it begin? How has it benefited you? How has it harmed you? For instance, is your only identity that of a fat person, struggling to lose weight? Who would you be if you lost the weight? Is it easier to be a "weight loss failure" than a "weight loss success?" How well do you handle success?

3. Tap out the top 7 statements.

4. As you were tapping out the statements, did you have any flashback or memories of the past, any additional insights, and/or ah-ha thoughts? If so, write them down. Make note of them.

521 – 540 EFT Tapping Statements

Experience is a hard teacher. She gives the test first, the lesson afterwards.
Vernon Sanders Law

521. I am not willing to sacrifice now for a possible return in the future.

522. I am sad that I don't have the willpower needed to lose the weight.

523. I am not willing to do the physical movement part of being healthy.

524. I don't have the self-discipline to maintain my weight loss program.

525. I am not willing to take the time necessary to lose weight correctly.

526. I am embarrassed by the excess weight I carry everywhere with me.

527. I am not willing to do the work required to lose weight permanently.

528. I lack the serious commitment needed to improve my life and health.

529. I am angry that others don't take me seriously because of my weight.

530. I am sad that no one takes me seriously because of my excess weight.

531. My weight has prevented me from _____.

532. My weight has prevented me from doing _____.

533. I am angry that people make judgments about me because of my weight.

534. I am not able to motivate myself over the long haul to improve my health.

535. I am sad that my weight has prevented me from having my hearts desires.

536. I am sad that I haven't live the life I wanted because of this excess weight.

537. I am angry that I have to deprive myself of the foods I love to lose weight.

538. My weight has prevented me from having what I thought I would have had.

539. My weight has prevented me from living the life I thought I would have lived.

540. I can't deal with the sexual attention I would get if I weighed my ideal weight.

Journaling Pages for Statements 521 - 540

We can have the results we say we want or we can have all the reasons why we cannot have them. We cannot have both. Reasons or results. We get to choose.

Susan Carlson

1. From the tapping statements between 1 – 20, list the top seven statements that you thought or felt applied to you:

1.

2.

3.

4.

5.

6.

7.

2. From this list of seven statements, select one and describe how it plays out in your life. Give an example or two. It is important to recognize and identify the pattern. Is there a trigger? How does it begin? How has it benefited you? How has it harmed you? For instance, are you embarrassed by the excess weight you carry everywhere with you? Embarrassment is actually anger. Is it okay to be angry at yourself? We don't take action until we are finally fed up? Embarrassment must not be enough for you to take action. If not, what would be?

3. Tap out the top 7 statements.

4. As you were tapping out the statements, did you have any flashback or memories of the past, any additional insights, and/or ah-ha thoughts? If so, write them down. Make note of them.

Food Cravings

Bread
Chocolate
Crunchy Foods
Dairy
Fatty/Fried Foods
Salty Foods
Spicy Foods
Sweets

Food Cravings

Our food cravings are trying to tell us something and it's not about the foods.

* Craving sweets might indicate a lack of joy in our lives.
* Craving crunchy foods might be an indication of frustration we are feeling.
* Craving bread might be an attempt to fill emptiness in our lives.

Food Cravings are symptoms. They are not the issue. Food cravings are symptoms of deeper issues in our lives. They are indications of what we need to heal.

The only way to truly end food cravings is to heal the cause.

To heal our food cravings we have to recognize, acknowledge, address, desensitize, and/or delete the thoughts, emotions, and memories that propel us toward the foods we crave.

Healing begins with an awareness of our actions and an understanding of the triggers that lead to the action. Knowing the significance of our food cravings can provide insights into what we really are craving.

To heal our food cravings, we need to heal the underlying cause... our dysfunctional beliefs and emotions.

BREAD

EMOTIONAL SIGNIFICANCE OF BREAD:

* An attempt to soothe tension, stress, and/or anxiety.
* Wanting to fill an inner emptiness.
* Looking for calm and comfort; reassurance.
* Feeling unsatisfied with life.
* A desire to ease pain.
* A desire to slow down.
* Calming and relaxing.

EFT TAPPING STATEMENTS FOR BREAD:

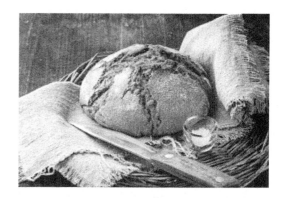

1. I like the feeling of being full.
2. I don't feel secure in the world.
3. My life is not satisfying or fulfilling.
4. I don't know how to find fulfillment.
5. I don't know what is missing in my life.
6. I crave bread when I am disappointed.
7. Eating bread fills the void I feel inside.
8. Bread is comforting when I feel lonely.
9. Bread is comforting when I feel empty.
10. I crave bread when I need reassurance.
11. I crave bread when I feel overwhelmed.
12. I can't get through a day without bread.
13. Bread is comforting when I am stressed.
14. There is something missing from my life.
15. I don't know what I need to feel fulfilled.
16. I can't keep up with everything in my life.
17. I crave bread when I want to be nurtured.
18. I crave bread when I want to be comforted.
19. I am totally addicted and attached to bread.
20. I crave bread when I am anxious and worried.
21. I eat bread when I feel overwhelmed with life.
22. I don't have the tools and skill to handle stress.
23. I want a guarantee that everything will work out.
24. I don't have the tools and skills to manage my anxiety.
25. There is not enough time to get everything accomplished.

CHOCOLATE

EMOTIONAL SIGNIFICANCE OF CHOCOLATE:

* Craving for love, intimacy, and/or romance.
* A need for calm.
* To lift one's mood, a "feel-good" boost.
* Looking for energy, passion, and/or excitement.
* Used as an anti-depressant.
* Unable to process sadness and grief.

EFT TAPPING STATEMENTS FOR CHOCOLATE:

1. My life lacks passion.
2. I have given up on love.
3. I crave love and romance.
4. I'm not in love with my life.
5. I fantasize about chocolate.
6. I need chocolate to do my life.
7. I crave chocolate when I am sad.
8. Eating chocolate soothes my pain.
9. My life lacks intimacy and romance.

10. I crave chocolates when I am lonely.
11. Chocolate makes everything better.
12. Chocolate makes everything A-okay.
13. I crave chocolate when I feel rejected.
14. I feel guilty when I indulge in chocolate.
15. I need chocolate to get through the day.
16. Chocolate gives me energy to do my life.
17. I crave chocolate when I don't feel loved.
18. The world melts away when I eat chocolate.
19. I need chocolate to handle the stresses of life.
20. I crave chocolate when I feel alone in the world.
21. Chocolate replaces the intimacy I lack in my life.
22. I crave chocolate to soothe my disappointments.
23. My day feels incomplete if I don't have chocolate.
24. I treat myself with chocolate when I want a reward.
25. Chocolate is one of my greatest source of pleasure.

CRUNCHY/CRISPY

EMOTIONAL SIGNIFICANCE OF CRUNCHY/CRISPY:

* An attempt to relieve anger, irritation, anxiety, and frustration.
* Stress relief.
* Lack "texture" in our lives.
* Longing for comfort and reassurance.
* Might be about anxiety, grief, sadness, depression, insecurity, regret, fear, self-doubt and/or shame.

EFT TAPPING STATEMENTS FOR CRUNCHY/CRISPY:

1. I am not my priority in life.
2. Crunching relieves my stress.
3. I get angry when I feel criticized.
4. I have a tendency to be impatient.
5. I am critical of myself and/or others.
6. I get impatient and/or annoyed easily.
7. I crave crunchy foods when I am angry.

8. I don't know how to heal my depression.
9. There is no one in my life to comfort me.
10. It is not okay or safe to express my anger.
11. I crave crunchy foods when I feel anxious.
12. I have a lot of anxiety, fear, and self-doubt.
13. I have a tendency to be anxious and worry.
14. I am angry I don't make my needs a priority.
15. I hide my anger, bitterness, and resentment.
16. I'm sad that this is the best my life will ever be.
17. I don't know what to do with the sadness I feel.
18. I crave crunchy foods when I need reassurance.
19. My life didn't turn out as I had thought it would.
20. I'm not sure I am living the life I want to be living.
21. I crave crunchy foods when I am feeling insecure.
22. I don't know how to heal my shame and self-doubt.
23. I crave crunchy foods when I feel I am being judged.
24. I am embarrassed when I am the center of attention.
25. I eat crunchy foods when someone finds fault with me.

Dairy
(Cheese, Ice Cream, Milk, Pudding, Creamy and Smooth)

Emotional Significance of Dairy:

* A craving for comfort.
* A yearning for being nurtured.
* Needing soothing.
* Looking for safety and security.
* To manage depression.
* To ease worry and anxiety.
* Feeling life is very tough and turbulent.
* Desire for life to be a little easier.

EFT Tapping Statements for Dairy:

1. Dairy soothes me.
2. Ice cream is comforting.
3. My life is constant chaos.
4. Dairy feels like mom's love.
5. Dairy eases my depression.
6. I don't take care of my needs.
7. I crave comfort and nurturing.
8. I crave dairy when I feel unsafe.
9. Life is very tough and turbulent.
10. I feel comforted when I eat dairy.
11. I crave dairy when I feel insecure.
12. I crave dairy when my life is tough.
13. I crave dairy when I feel burdened.
14. I crave dairy when I feel depressed.
15. I crave dairy when my life is chaotic.
16. I crave dairy when life is unbearable.
17. Dairy makes me feel safe and secure.
18. I crave dairy when I am in overwhelm.
19. I crave dairy when I feel overwhelmed.
20. I crave dairy when I wish life was easier.
21. I want someone else to take care of me.
22. I crave dairy when the going gets tough.
23. I crave dairy when my life lacks nurturing.
24. I crave dairy when I feel worried and anxious.
25. I am craving smoothness and softness in my life.

Fatty / Fried Foods

(Fried Foods, Ice Cream, High-fat Dairy)

Emotional Significance of Fatty Foods:

* Fills the emptiness.
* Feeling unsatisfied, unfulfilled, and/or empty.
* Yearning for the richness of life.
* A lack of inspiration in life.
* Lacking self-esteem and self-worth.
* Desire to accept our own authenticity.

EFT Tapping Statements for Fatty/Fried Foods:

1. My life lacks meaning.
2. My life lacks "richness."
3. I play my life small and safe.
4. My life will never be fulfilling.
5. It is difficult to accept myself.
6. I yearn for the richness of life.
7. My self-esteem is non-existent.
8. My desires are out of my reach.
9. My life is unfulfilling and empty.
10. My needs will never be fulfilled.
11. I have nothing important to offer.
12. I don't know what would fulfill me.
13. I eat fried foods when I feel unworthy.
14. I lack inspiration to live a meaningful life.
15. I don't know how to overcome my apathy.
16. I eat fatty foods when my life feels empty.
17. I eat fatty foods when I want to escape life.
18. It is hopeless I will ever achieve my desires.
19. I will never accomplish anything worthwhile.
20. I don't have the courage to pursue my dreams.
21. I don't know how to heal my emotional wounds.
22. I don't have the courage to be my authentic self.
23. I crave fatty/fried foods when I feel I have no worth.
24. I crave fatty/fried foods when I feel less than others.
25. I crave fatty/fried foods when I yearn for the richness of life.

Salty Foods

Emotional Significance of Salty:

* A desire for grounding, stability, and/or security.
* A lack of flow in our lives.
* A need for down time and relaxation.
* "Salt of the earth."
* Might be about stress, anger, anxiety.
* Desire to heal emotional stagnation.
* Desire to let go of stress.
* Desire to release emotions.

EFT Tapping Statements for Salty:

1. My comfort zone is a rut.
2. I never have time to just be.
3. I am not grounded or stable.
4. I yearn for stability in my life.
5. I don't know how to handle stress.
6. My life lacks stability and security.
7. I don't know how to live in the flow.
8. I am only safe when my life is stable.
9. It is not comfortable for me to relax.
10. I crave salty foods when I am stressed.
11. I crave salty foods when I feel anxious.
12. I am anxious when my life lacks security.
13. I am fearful of moving into the unknown.
14. I am unable to deal with emotional stress.
15. I blame myself for all the wrong in my life.
16. I am safe only when I ignore my emotions.
17. It not okay or safe to express my emotions.
18. I crave salty foods when I feel ungrounded.
19. I don't know how to go with the flow of life.
20. I don't know how to heal my emotional pain.
21. I crave salty food when life is overwhelming.
22. I don't know how to create stability in my life.
23. I don't know how to replenish what I have lost.
24. I can't move forward in my life without stability.
25. I crave salty food when I feel life is out of control.

Spicy Foods

Emotional Significance of Spicy:

* A craving and drive for intensity and excitement.
* Searching for passion.
* Response to boredom.
* Wanting more adventure.
* Looking for action in our lives.
* Wanting to "spice up" our life.
* Wanting more variety in our life.
* Wanting more in life and out of life.

EFT Tapping Statements for Spicy:

1. I crave excitement.
2. I am bored with my life.
3. My life lacks excitement.
4. My life is dull and mundane.
5. I crave more spice in my life.
6. I crave more variety in my life.
7. I am stuck in a monotonous rut.
8. My life is boring and unexciting.
9. I have nothing to look forward to.
10. I do the same thing day after day.
11. I feel alive when I eat spicy foods.
12. I crave more excitement in my life.
13. I crave spicy food when I am bored.
14. I want more of everything in my life.
15. I have given up on adventure and fun.
16. I'm frustrated that my life is so boring.
17. My passions are nowhere to be found.
18. I don't deserve to have the life I desire.
19. My dreams are too grand to be fulfilled.
20. I crave the excitement that risks provide.
21. Eating spicy foods adds variety to my life.
22. Eating spicy foods adds "spice" to my life.
23. I crave spicy food when I crave excitement.
24. Eating spicy foods spices up my boring life.
25. I thought life would be more exciting than it is.

SWEETS
(CANDY, DONUTS, PASTRIES, CAKE, COOKIES, ICE CREAM)

EMOTIONAL SIGNIFICANCE OF SWEETS:

* A craving for sweetness in life.
* A lack of joy in life.
* Wanting a reward.
* Seeking pleasure.
* Don't feel "sweet" enough.
* Needing a boost of energy.
* Feeling exhausted.

EFT TAPPING STATEMENTS FOR SWEETS:

1. I am not sweet enough.
2. My life lacks sweetness.
3. My joy is nowhere to be found.
4. Sweets get me through the day.
5. I don't create enough "me" time.
6. I fantasize about sweets all day long.
7. Sweets lift me up when I am dragging.
8. I could eat endless amounts of sweets.
9. I deserve a sweet reward for all that I do.
10. I crave sweets when I want to reward myself.
11. I don't know how to face my sadness and hurt.
12. I don't know how to heal my sadness and hurt.
13. I feel deprived if I don't have something sweet.
14. I eat sweets when I am feeling sorry for myself.
15. It is hopeless that I will ever have the life I want.
16. I indulge in sweets to numb my disappointments.
17. My day is incomplete if I don't have anything sweet.
18. I don't have enough energy to accomplish all my goals.
19. I acknowledge my accomplishments with a sweet treat.
20. Eating sweets is the only way I can get through the day.
21. It is hopeless that I will ever resolve my hurt and sadness.
22. There isn't enough time in the day for my needs to be met.
23. It is hopeless that my life will be any different than it is now.
24. The only thing I have to look forward to is my sweet reward.
25. It feels like something is missing if I don't have a sweet treat.

Books by Tessa Cason

All Things EFT Tapping Manual

* Why does EFT Tapping work for some and not for others?
* How do you personalize EFT Tapping to be most effective for you?
* What is the very first tapping statement you need to tap?

This manual provides instructions on how to heal our disappointments, regrets, and painful memories.

EFT Tapping information has instructions on what to do if a tapping statement does not clear, what to do if tapping doesn't work for you, and how to write your own tapping statements.

We must eliminate the dysfunctional beliefs if we want to make changes in our lives. EFT Tapping can do just that. EFT Tapping is a simple, yet very powerful tool to heal our beliefs, emotions, painful memories, and stories.

500 EFT Tapping Statements for Moving Out of Survival

Survival is stress on steroids. It's feeling anxious and not good enough. Survival may be the most important topic we can heal within ourselves. Survival is programmed into our DNA.

Ella returned home from the market with her three year old daughter to find a note from her husband that he did not want to be married any longer. Under the note were divorce papers, the number of the divorce attorney, and $500.

Wanting to be able to give her daughter a wonderful childhood, she had to figure out how to survive and thrive. This is her story and the tapping statements she tapped.

Dr. John Montgomery says, "All 'negative,' or distressing, emotions, like fear, disgust, or anxiety, can be thought of as 'survival-mode' emotions: they signal that our survival and well-being may be at risk."

80 EFT Tapping Statements for Change

If it is not okay or safe for our lives to change, every time our lives change, the body is subjected to a tremendous amount of stress.

After graduating from high school, Charlie's dad told Charlie he could continue to live at home, but he would be charged room and board. At 18, Charlie was now financially responsible for himself. He was able to find a job and moved out.

Within a year, circumstances forced Charlie to move back home. Day after day, Charlie rode the bus to work. After work, he rode the bus home. One day as Charlie was riding the bus to work, he noticed another regular rider, Dan, tapping his head.

Together Dan and Charlie began tapping. Find out the results of their tapping and the statements they tapped.

300 EFT Tapping Statements for Self-defeating Behaviors, Victim, Self-pity

Tom had lots of excuses and reasons for his lack of "results." His boss, Robert MacGregor, saw the potential Tom had and asked his longtime friend, Sam Anderson, a life coach, to work with Tom. Read Tom's story to understand how Tom was able to step into his potential.

Self defeating behaviors take us away from our goals, from what we want, leaving us feeling exhausted, disempowered, and defeated. Self defeating thoughts are the negative thoughts we have about ourselves and/or the world around us such as "I'm not good enough", "I have to be perfect to be accepted."

Most likely, you have tried to change the self-defeating and self sabotage behavior, yet here you are with the same patterns.

100 EFT Tapping Statements for Feeling Fulfilled

John wasn't sure what would fulfill him. He loved his job and didn't want to find a new career, but he wasn't feeling fulfilled in his life. With the help of his wife, John found what would be fulfilling.

100 EFT Tapping Statements™ for Feeling Fulfilled
Tessa Cason

Fulfillment is a simple formula, actually. It's the follow-through that might be the problem.

What would prevent you from being fulfilled? Do you know what the blocks might be, the reason you remain out of sync, unfulfilled? Is it about leaving your comfort zone or maybe it's that you allow your limitations to define your life?

It is possible to remove the blocks, heal the beliefs on the subconscious level, and move toward your desire for fulfillment. To do so, we need a powerful tool. One such tool is EFT Tapping, the Emotional Freedom Technique.

100 EFT Tapping Statements for Being Extraordinary!

Being Extraordinary

100 EFT Tapping Statements™ for Being Extraordinary!
Tessa Cason

Accomplishing extraordinary performances, having incredible successes, or earning large sums of money does not equate to an extraordinary person. This book is about discovering your extraordinary character.

Extraordinary – Exceeding ordinary, beyond ordinary.

Extraordinary starts with the self, our character, depth, and strength of our being. It's being congruent, walking our talk. It is the love, compassion, and tenderness we show ourselves. It's the pure and highest essence of our being.

Rebecca was approaching a time in her life in which she was doing some soul searching and examining her life. She didn't feel extraordinary. In her late 50s, she felt she was just ordinary. She reached out to Tessa. The email exchanges are included in this book along with tapping statements.

400 EFT Tapping Statements for Being Empowered and Successful

Empowered and Successful

400 EFT Tapping Statements™ for Being Empowered and Successful
Tessa Cason

Being empowered is not about brute strength or the height of our successes. It is the strength, substance, and character of our inner being. It is knowing that whatever life throws at us, we will prevail.

Ava has just started a business with her two very successful sisters. She wants the business with her sisters to succeed, yet, she doesn't feel empowered. She doesn't want to feel as if the business would fail because of her and is ready to do the emotional work so she matches her sisters' power and success.

Sophie, Ava's roommate and an EFT practitioner-in-training, works with Ava. With Sophie's help, Ava begins to feel empowered and that her business with her sisters will be a success.

300 EFT Tapping Statements for Healing the Self

Healing the Self

300 EFT Tapping Statements for Healing the Self
Tessa Cason

We live in a complex world with multiple influences. At birth, it starts with our parents and soon afterwards, the influence of other family members (grandparents, siblings, etc.), TV shows, cartoon characters, commercials, and peers. As we get older, we have the influences of teachers, coaches, tutors, television and movie stars, pop stars, sports heroes, and so many other.

When Pete was offered a promotion at work and was not excited about something he had worked so hard to accomplish, he knew he needed to find some answers. He thought he was living his mother's version of his life. He didn't know what brought him joy.

With the help of EFT and an EFT Practitioner, Pete was able to discover his version of his life, what brought him joy, and how to live a fulfilling life.

EFT Tapping for Anxiety, Fear, Anger, Self Pity, Courage (1,000 Tapping Statements)

Anxiety is a combination of 4 things: Unidentified Anger, Hurt, Fear, and Self Pity. We expect error, rejection, humiliation, and actually start to anticipate it.

When we are not in present time, we are either in the past or the future. Anger is the past. Fear is the future. Fear could actually be anger that we failed in the past and most likely will fail again in the future.

It takes courage on our part to heal the anxiety, identify the hurt, and to give up the self-pity. To heal, to thrive, and flourish, we need to address not only the Anxiety, but also the fear, anger, self pity, and hurt.

Healing is not about managing symptoms. It's about alleviating the cause of the symptoms.

80 EFT Tapping Statements for Feeling Less Than and Anxiety

Rene was excited for the year long mentoring program she enrolled in. *How wonderful*, she thought, *to be surrounded with like-minded people.* Five months into the program, she abruptly dropped out. Find out how her feeling Less Than and her Anxiety sabotaged her personal growth.

Anxiety has four parts: unidentified anger, hurt, fear, and self-pity. Living in a state of fear, we want a guarantee that our decisions and choices will produce the results or outcomes that we want. Feeling less than is played out in a cycle of shame, hopelessness, and self-pity. We feel shame about who we are, that we have little value, and that we are not good enough.

Feeling "less than" spirals down into depression, survival, and self-sabotage.

240 EFT Tapping Statements for Fear

Two months before school ended, Lennie was downsized from as a high school music teacher. When he was unable to find another job, fear crept into his thoughts. What if he couldn't find a job in music again? He wasn't qualified to do anything different. He was scared that he would not be able to support his family and they would end up homeless. He could feel the fear as his stomach was in knots.

Fear is that sense of dread, knots in the stomach, chill that runs down our spine, and the inability to breathe. We all know it. Fight-Flight-Freeze.

Fear is a self-protection mechanism. It is an internal alarm system that alerts us to potential harm. When we are in present time, we have the courage, awareness, wisdom, discernment, and confidence to identify and handle that which could cause us harm.

80 EFT Tapping Statements for Anxiety and Worry

"I just can't do this anymore," said Frank to his wife Mary. "You worry about everything. When we got married, your anxiety was something you did every now and then. But now you are paranoid about everything. I leave for work and you act like you are never going to see me again."

Anxiety is a combination of 4 things: unidentified anger, hurt, fear, self-pity. We expect error, rejection, humiliation, and actually start to anticipate it. It is an internal response to a perceived threat to our well-being. We feel threatened by an abstract, unknown danger that could harm us in the future.

Worry is a mild form of anxiety. Worry is a tendency to mull over and over and over anxiety-provoking thoughts. Worry is thinking, in an obsessive way, about something that has happened or will happen. Going over something again and again and asking, "What will I do? What should I have done?"

200 ET Tapping Statements for Healing a Broken Heart

She found someone who made her feel cherished, valued, and loved. Tall, dark, and handsome as well as aware, present and understanding. Matt was an awesome guy. He thought she, too, was someone special, intriguing, and awesome.

Matt was promoted at work which meant months away from home and thus, decided to end their relationship. Her best friend introduced her to EFT Tapping to heal her broken heart.

Time does not heal all. Healing the grief of a broken heart is not easy. Grief is more than sadness. Grief is a loss. Something of value is gone. Grief is an intense loss that breaks our hearts.

Over time, unhealed grief becomes anger, blame, resentment, and/or remorse. To heal a broken heart, we need to identify, acknowledge, and healed the dysfunctional beliefs. EFT Tapping can help.

400 EFT Tapping Statements for Dealing with Emotions

Did you see the movie Pleasantville with Tobey Maguire and Reese Witherspoon, two siblings who are trapped in a 1950s black and white TV show, set in a small midwest town where everything is seemingly perfect. David and Jennifer (Tobey and Reese) must pretend they are Bud and Mary Sue Parker, the son and daughter in the TV show.

Slowly, the town begins changing from black and white to color as the townspeople begin to experience emotions. Experiencing emotions is like adding color to a black and white movie. Color adds a depth, enjoyment, and pleasure to the movie. Emotions add depth, enjoyment, and pleasure to our lives.

Emotions add animation, richness, and warmth to our lives. They give our lives meaning and fullness. Without emotions, our lives would be as boring as watching a black and white movie.

80 EFT Tapping Statements for Abandonment

Feelings of abandonment can be triggered by the ending of a relationship as well as the death of an individual. Even though we may have an intellectual understanding of death, there is still a feeling of abandonment when someone we treasure dies. For a small child, they do not understand death. They may still expect the parent to return at any time.

Even though Kevin drove an expensive sports car he wasn't the playboy type. He wanted to settle down and start a family. Kevin felt Susan could be "the one." He wanted to talk to her about taking their relationship to the next level.

Before Kevin could talk to Susan, she ended the relationship because of his insecurities in their relationship. She felt it had to do with the abandonment of his mom when he was a child. This book gives you the exact statements that Kevin tapped to deal with his insecurities in relationships.

EFT Tapping Statements for A Broken Heart: Abandonment, Anger, Depression, Grief, Emotional Healing (1,000 Statements)

Time does not heal all. When our hearts have been shattered, we feel nothing will ever be the same again. We are flooded with emotions... anger, grief, depression...

Regardless of what led to the broken heart, maybe a death, divorce, or a breakup, the result is the same...a broken heart. To heal a broken heart is not only about healing the grief, but also the feelings of abandonment, anger, and depression.

Being abandoned is a verb. It is something that "happens to us." The result of being abandoned is anger, grief, and depression. Grief is the sadness we experience when we have lost something of value.

In order to heal, we need to resolve the anger, grief, abandonment, and depression that resulted from our hearts being fractured.

200 ET Tapping Statements for Wealth

After graduating from high school, Amy looked for a job for a solid year unsuccessfully! She lacked the necessary experience and education. She felt like she was in a vicious cycle, going round and round and round. Finally, she was hired at a large chain store. For the last eight years, she has been shuffled, unhappily, between different departments.

As a birthday gift, her mom gave her a session with an EFT Practitioner to determine what she wanted to do with her life. Follow along with Amy on her journey to self-discovery.

What we manifest in our lives is a direct result of our beliefs. If we have a mentality of wealth and abundance, we will prosper and thrive.

Our beliefs determine the level of our wealth and abundance. To heal our dysfunctional beliefs, we need a powerful tool. EFT Tapping is one such tool.

EFT Tapping Statements for Prosperity, Survival, Courage, Personal Power, Success
(1,000 Statements)

What we believe determines our prosperity. Our beliefs determine our thoughts and feelings which in turn determine our choices and decisions. Therefore, what we manifest in our lives is a direct result of our beliefs. If we are happy and joyful, we will see happiness in everything. If we are fearful, we will see fear around every corner. If we have a mentality of abundance, we will prosper.

It is difficult to be prosperous when we are stuck in survival. In survival, we feel disempowered to thrive. We can only survive. It takes Courage to step into our Personal Power and to Succeed. We need a powerful tool to heal our dysfunctional beliefs. EFT Tapping is one such tool.

In this book, there are 200 tapping statements for each of these 5 topics - Prosperity, Survival, Courage, Personal Power, and Success.

80 EFT Tapping Statements for Abundance, Wealth, Money

Abby just had her 46th birthday. She tried to celebrate but she didn't have anything to be happy about. Her parents had died in a car accident the Christmas before while driving home from her new home after celebrating Christmas. Both of her parents were real estate agents. She was their transaction coordinator. The three of them had their own offices, handling any real estate transaction that someone might need. Without them, she had no real estate transactions to coordinate.

Abby funds were running dry. She had applied for jobs without success. Abby talked to every one she and her parents knew in hopes of finding a job. With the slow real estate market, she was unable to find any work.

Find out how Abby turned her life around and the exact statements that Abby tapped to deal with her monetary issues.

400 EFT Tapping Statements for Dreams to Reality

Have you done everything you were supposed to do for your dreams to become reality? You were clear on what they were. You made your vision boards with lots of pictures of what you desired. You visualized them coming true and living that life. You've stated your affirmations over and over and over for their fulfillment. You released and allowed the Universe to handle the details. And, now, dust is collecting on your vision boards and you are still waiting for the Universe to handle the details.

Our dreams are our hopes and desires of what we want to come true one day. They are snapshots of what we want our future to be. Yet, sometimes, maybe most of the time, our dreams do not become reality and never manifest themselves in our lives. We gave up on our dreams a long time ago.

Jane shares her story of how she used EFT Tapping to turn her dreams into reality.

300 ET Tapping Statements for Intuition

Quinn was one of Tessa's students in her Developing Your Intuition class. She had been hesitant to develop her intuition. One of her basic needs was Belonging. If she was intuitive, she might not belong and thus, realized this was part of her hesitation.

She also had a tendency to avoid which also wasn't conductive to developing her intuition. Tessa wrote out some EFT Tapping statements for her to tap:
* I ignore my inner voice.
* No one I know uses intuition.
* I'm too logical to be intuitive.
* Being intuitive is too complicated.

Included in this book are exercises and helpful hints to develop your intuition as well info on Symbolism, Colors, Number, Charkas, Asking Questions of Our Intuition, Archetypes, and 36 Possible Reasons We Took Physical Form.

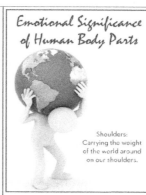

Emotional Significance of Human Body Parts.Chasing the Pain

"We carry the weight of the world around on our shoulders." The emotional significance of the shoulder is about responsibility

The body "talks" to us...in its language. To understand what the body is saying, we need to learn the body's language.

Jona greeted me at the airport gate on crutches. After hugging each other, she asked what the left ankle meant. I told her the left side of the body had to do with what's going on in the inside and the ankles had to do with commitments.

She had been dating a man for the last two months and he just proposed.

Chasing the Pain is a technique with EFT Tapping that as we tap for a physical pain we are experiencing, the original pain might disappear only to be felt in a different part of the body.

100 EFT Tapping Statements for Accepting Our Uniqueness and Being Different

Brian was an intelligent high school student with average grades. He tested high on all the assessment tests. Brian didn't think of himself as intelligent since his grades were only average. He didn't plan on going to college because he thought he wasn't smart enough and would flunk out.

His counselor knew otherwise and suggested Brian retake the tests to see if the tests were wrong. Find out Brian's scores after he retook the tests and how Mr. Cole introduced EFT Tapping to Brian.

If you were your unique self, do you fear being alone, rejected, or labeled as "undesirable?" Or maybe it's being laughed at and ridiculed for being different and unique?

When we play our lives safe, we end up feeling angry, anxious, powerless, hopeless, and depressed.

Muscle Testing.Obstacles and Helpful Hints

Muscle testing is a method in which we can converse with the subconscious mind as well as the body's nervous system and energy field.

This book details 10 obstacles and 10 helpful hints to successfully muscle test.

One obstacle is that it is a necessity that the tester be someone that calibrates the same, or above, that of the testee, on David Hawkins' Map of Consciousness or be in the higher altitudes, 250 or higher, on the Map.

Helpful hint: When muscle testing, the tester and testee should not make eye contact with each other. With eye contact, the answer would be "our" energy instead of the "testee's" energy.

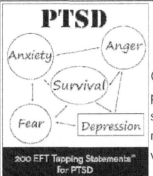

200 ET Tapping Statements for PTSD

George believed that if he prepared for his death, it was signaling the Universe he was ready to die. George did die without preparing his wife.

George took care of everything. The only thing Helen had to take care of George.

After George died, she had no idea if they owned the home they lived in, if George had life insurance, how to pay bills, if they had money, if they did, where was it? She didn't know if George had left a will. She was not prepared for George's death or how to take care of everything that George took care of.

With the help of friends and EFT Tapping, Helen was able to heal and learn how to take care of everything that George once did.

Healing is not about managing symptoms. It is about alleviating the cause of the symptoms.

EFT Tapping Statements for PTSD, Survival, Disempowered, Fear, Anger (1,200 Statements)

The potential exists for anyone that is in any life threatening situation in which they fear for their life, that believes death is imminent, to experience PTSD.

With PTSD, our Survival is at stake. As a result of our survival being threatened, we feel Disempowered to thrive. We can only survive. When we are caught in Survival, Fear is a prevalent emotion. When we feel Disempowered, Anger is just beneath the surface.

To heal, to thrive, and flourish, we need to address not only the PTSD, but also Survival and Feeling Disempowered, Fear, and Anger. (Thus, the 5 topics in this PTSD Workbook.)

Healing PTSD is a process in which we must desensitize, decrease, and heal the survival response. EFT Tapping is the best method to do so.

200 EFT Tapping Statements for Conflict

"Hi, Julia. So glad you called." Excitedly, I said, "I just finished decorating the house and I'm ready for Christmas!"

Not at all thrilled to be talking to her sister-on-law, Julia said, "That's why I'm calling. You don't mind if I host the family Christmas get-together, do you?"

A little surprised, I said, "Well, I do.

"Tough," she said. "I'm hosting Christmas this year."

This wasn't the first "conflict" with her sister-in-law. But, Audrey was a conflict coward and did not engage.

After EFT Tapping, Audrey overcame her issues with conflict. Find out how and who hosted Christmas that year!

80 EFT Tapping Statements for Anger

Doug was immensely proud of his son, Andy, until he watched his son (a high school senior) jeopardize his chance at an athletic scholarship to attend college. The count was 3-2, three balls and two strikes. The final pitch was thrown and Andy let it go by. The umpire shouts, "Strike!" Andy has just struck out.

"What's wrong with your eyes old man?" Andy shouts at the umpire. "That was a ball. It wasn't in the strike zone. Need instant replay so you can see it in slow motion? I'm not out!"

Andy, was following his father's example of being a rageaholic. EFT Tapping helped both Doug and Andy to take control of his life and his anger.

Anger is not right or wrong, healthy or unhealthy. It is the expression of anger that makes it right or wrong, healthy or unhealthy.

400 ET Tapping Statements for Being a Champion

Jack was a professional runner that injured himself at the US Championships. He was unable to compete at the World Championship. The previous year, Jack had won gold at the World Championships. After six months, he still was not able to run even though the doctors assured him he should be able to run. He had exhausted all medical and physical therapy treatments without success or hope of being able to run pain-free.

Our of frustration, Jack decided to look at the mental piece with a transformation coach. Follow Jack's recovery back to the track through EFT Tapping.

Champions are rare. If being a champion was easy then everyone would be a champion and a champion would not be anything special. It is in the difficulty of the task that, once accomplished, makes a champion great.

EFT Tapping Statements for Champion, Personal Power, Success, Self Confidence, Role Model (1,000 Statements)

Being a champion is more than just being successful. It is the achievement of excellence. It is more than just being competent. It is about stepping into one's power. It is more than just setting goals. It is the achievement of those goals with perseverance, dedication, and determination. It is not just about the practicing, training, and learning. It is the application and implementation of the training and learning into a competition and into everyday situations.

Champions are successful, but not all successful people are champions. Champions are powerful, but not all powerful people are champions. Champions are confident but not all confident people are champions. Champions dream big but not all people that dream big are champions.

300 EFT Tapping Statements for Dealing with Obnoxious People

Three siblings were each dealing with an obnoxious person in their lives. Katherine was dealing with a co-worker that took credit for her accomplishments.

Megan, a professional athlete, was distracted by a narcissistic team member that disrupted practice and thus, her performances at meets.

Peter was a very successful college student that had a Teaching Assistant jealous of everything that Peter was and the TA was not.

Read how each resolved and solved their issue with an obnoxious person.

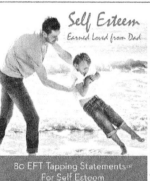

80 EFT Tapping Statements for Self Esteem

Ron had driven a semi-trailer truck for 30 years for the same company. To celebrate his 60th birthday and 30 years of service, his company had a celebration for him. After the celebration, Ron's boss suggested that he find a job that was more age appropriate. Ron's lack of self-esteem was interfering with moving on with his life. This book gives you the exact statements that Ron tapped to heal his lack of self esteem, self respect, and self-pride.

From birth to about the age of seven, we learn self love from mom. From about the age of seven through twelve, from dad we learn self esteem, earned loved. Self esteem is about the feelings, respect, and pride we have in ourselves.

The lack of self esteem shows up in our lives as a lack self respect and/or pride in ourselves. This "lack" will taint every area of our lives.

340 ET Tapping Statements for Healing From the Loss of a Loved One

Grief is more than sadness. It is more than unhappiness. Grief is a loss. Something of value is gone. Grief is an intense loss that breaks our heart. Loss can be the death of a loved one, a pet, a way of life, a job, a marriage, one's own imminent death. Grief is real.

Over time, unhealed grief becomes anger, resentment, blame, and/or remorse. We become someone that we are not. It takes courage to move through the grief and all the emotions buried deep within.

John's father died of a heart attack while gardening. A year after his death, John still was not able to move on or be happy. His wife handed him a business card of an EFT Practitioner and recommended therapy to heal the grief. After working with the Practitioner, John was able to find his joy again.

100 EFT Tapping Statements for Feeling Deserving

Sarah, a sophomore in college, was unsure of what to declare as her major. She met with a guidance counselor who wanted to chat first.

Sarah thought of herself as an accident since she had two older siblings who had already moved out of the house when she was five. Her parents had been looking forward to an empty nest, instead, they had a third child that was just starting school.

Sarah had felt undeserving her whole life, even though her parents loved her dearly and never treated her life an accident.

Travel the path Sarah walked with the counselor to finally feel deserving.

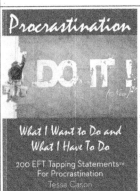

200 EFT Tapping Statements for Procrastination.What I Want to Do and What I Have to Do

Procrastination is about avoiding.
* What are we avoiding?
* What are we afraid to find out?
* What are we not wanting to do?
* What are we not willing to face?

Is it:
* We don't have the tools and skills to do something.
* Rebellion
* Lack of motivation.
* Not knowing what needs to be done.
* Poor time management.

The list is long why we procrastinate and what it could be about. What do we do to heal our procrastination tendencies? EFT Tapping. To heal we have to be able to recognize, acknowledge, and take ownership of that which we want to heal. Then we have to delete the dysfunctional beliefs on the subconscious level. EFT is one such tool that can do just that.

80 EFT Tapping Statements for Relationship with Self

Stephanie, now 55 years old, used to be excited about life and about her life. That was 35 years ago. She was engaged to the love of her life. A month before the wedding her fiancée ran off with a beauty queen.

After 35 years, Stephanie still felt defeated, beaten, defective, broken, and flawed. She was still resentful. She had become comfortable in apathy because she did not know how to move beyond her self-pity.

With the help of EFT Tapping, Stephanie was able to heal her wounded self and begin to live life again.

Do you feel disconnected from yourself? Do you feel as if you could never be whole? Do you feel defeated by life? To change our lives, we have to be able to recognize, acknowledge, and take ownership of that which we want to change. Then heal the dysfunctional beliefs on a subconscious level. EFT Tapping can help.

700 ET Tapping Statements for Weight, Emotional Eating, & Food Cravings

Emma's sister's wedding was fast approaching. She would be asked at the wedding how her diet was going.

Emma has struggled with her weight for the last 35 years, since high school. Out of desperation, Hannah began working with an EFT Practitioner. Follow her journey to healing the cause of her weight issues.

Excess weight, food cravings, emotional eating, and overeating are symptoms of deeper unresolved issues beneath the weight. Attempting to solve the problem by only dealing with the symptoms is ineffective and does not heal the issue.

Weight is the symptom. The usual programs for weight loss aren't working because they are attempting to solve the problem by dealing with the symptom instead of healing the cause.

EFT Tapping Statements for Weight + Food Cravings, Anger, Grief, Not Good Enough, Failure (1,150 Statements)

Excess weight, food cravings, emotional eating, and overeating are symptoms of deeper issues beneath the weight. Attempting to solve the problem by only dealing with the symptoms is ineffective and does not heal the issue.

The usual programs for weight loss aren't working because they are attempting to solve the problem by dealing with the symptom instead of healing the cause.

IF WE WANT TO HEAL OUR WEIGHT ISSUES, WE NEED TO HEAL THE CAUSE...THE DYSFUNCTIONAL BELIEFS AND EMOTIONS.

HEALING IS NOT ABOUT MANAGING SYMPTOMS. IT'S ABOUT ALLEVIATING THE CAUSE OF THE SYMPTOMS.

80 EFT Tapping Statements for Addictions

Derrick's mom died when he was a senior in high school. His dad (an alcoholic) told Derrick that as soon as he graduated from high school, he was on his own.

The day that Derrick graduated from high school, he went down and enlisted in the army. In the army, he started to drink. A month after his enlistment concluded, he met a wonderful woman. They married and had a child.

One day when Derrick returned home from the bar, he found an empty house and a note. The note told him that since has unwilling to admit he was an alcoholic or to go to counseling, she was left with only one choice. That choice was to relocate herself and their daughter to some place safe, away from him.

Derrick felt he had nothing to live for. He discovered someone at work that was a recovering alcoholic. She introduced her secret, EFT Tapping, to Derrick.

80 EFT Tapping Statements for Weight and Emotional Eating

Excess weight is a symptom, not the cause of overeating and emotional eating.

The day that Tracy was graduating from UCLA, she received a phone call that her father had fallen and had been hospitalized. She was on the next flight home to Dallas. It was decided that her father needed surgery and that Tracy should stay on for a short while to care for her dad. No one asked Tracy what she wanted. But, she stayed anyway.

Seven months later, even though her father had mended, Tracy had become her father's caregiver. This is not what Tracy had planned to do with her life after graduating from college. Every month, over the course of the seven unhappy months, Tracy's weight spiraled up, until she was at her highest weight EVER.

This book gives you the exact statements that Tracy tapped to heal the cause of her weight gain.

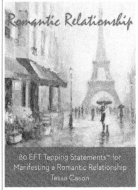

80 EFT Tapping Statements for Manifesting a Romantic Relationship

Tanya tells the story about her best friend, Nica. Nica wants a relationship. She wants to be in love, the happily-ever-after kind of love. Nica is self-absorbed, self-centered, smart, and pretty.

Nica has had several long-term relationships but, never allows anyone close enough to get to know her. When she is in between boyfriends, she always whines:

* No man will ever want me.
* The odds are slim to none that I will find anyone.
* I have a bad track record with men so I give up.
* There will never be anyone for me.
* My desires will never be fulfilled.

Tanya is a tapper and finally Nica agrees to do some tapping as a last resort! The Tapping Statements that Nica tapped to manifest a relationship are listed in this eBook.

80 EFT Tapping Statements for Social Anxiety

In social settings, Johnny felt very awkward. He did not enjoy the limelight or any attention focused on him at all!

"Dude," Johnny's buddies would say. "When are you going to get over this fear of talking to a woman?" Johnny would laugh off their comments.

Social Anxiety – Dreading, fearing, and/or expecting to be rejected and/or humiliated by others in social settings.

* A feeling of discomfort, fear, dread, or worry that is centered on our interactions with other people.
* Fear of being judged negatively by others.
* Fear of being evaluated negatively by others.

Is there hope for those that have social anxiety? Yes. EFT Tapping. Tap the statements that Johnny tapped to overcome his social anxiety.

80 EFT Tapping Statements for Adult Children of Alcoholics

Did you have a parent that was an alcoholic? Do you have difficulty relating and connecting to others? Do you have a strong need to be perfect? Is your self-esteem low and judge yourself harshly? Do you have a fear of abandonment and rejection? If so, then EFT Tapping might help.

Rebecca had lost her 4th job. She was defensive, argumentative, and resentful. Rebecca knew her boss was right in firing her.

Rebecca's childhood was anything but idyllic. Her father was a raging alcoholic. She was terrified of his anger. Rebecca tried to be perfect so her dad couldn't find fault with her. Home life was hell. She had to grow up really fast and was never allow to be a kid or to play.

Rebecca did see an EFT Practitioner and was able to heal the anger, the need to be perfect, and other issues one has when they have an alcoholic parent.

200 EFT Tapping Statements for Knowing God

So many questions surround this topic, God. Does God exist or is God a fabrication? Is God for real or just a concept? If God does exist, then what is God's role in our lives?

Do our prayers get answered or are we praying in vain? Does God make mistakes? God created Lucifer and then kicked out a third of his angels from heaven along with Lucifer. Was Lucifer a mistake and all the angels that choose to follow Lucifer? Do we just want to believe that a supreme being really cares about us, gave us our lives' purpose, a mission, and a destiny? God is as varied as there are people.

Many have said that God gave humans the power of choice and free will. If this is true, the consequences of our actions are ours alone. Yet, there are those who believe that God could intervene. God should take action to protect and provide for us.

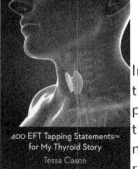

400 ET Tapping Statements for My Thyroid Story

In 2005, I was diagnosed with thyroid cancer. I researched the potential cause and discovered that 20 years after exposure to natural gas, thyroid issues will result. 20 years previous to the diagnosis, I lived in a townhouse for 850 days that had a gas leak.

While pursuing healing modalities after the exposure to natural gas, I began to realize that about 50% of our health issues are emotionally produced. The other 50% are the result of environmental factors such as smoking, chemicals, accidents, and/or hereditary.

I did not believe my emotional issues caused the thyroid cancer. It was the result of an environmental factor outside myself. BUT, since the thyroid was affected, if I worked on the emotional issues that had to do with the thyroid, it should impact the thyroid cancer. That was my theory.

100 EFT Tapping Statements for Fear of Computers

Can you image strapping on your Jet pack to get to work? Traveling on the Hyperloop that travels at speeds up to 600 mph to visit a friend that lives in another state? Stepping into your self-driving car that chauffeurs you to the restaurant? Soon all of these will be a part of our lives.

Modern technology! Most everyone knows that the computer can answer most any question. Most every job today and jobs of the future require at least some knowledge of computers.

Grandmere was intimidated by the computer. Her motivation was her granddaughter would was moving to another country. Granddaughter wants her to learn to use the computer so they can Skype when she is out of the country. Read how Grandmere was able to overcome her anxiety and fear of the computer.

200 EFT Tapping Statements for Sex

Is sex about the act or is sex about the intimacy shared by the act? Is sex about the orgasms or is it about the connection, touching, and cuddling?

In most culture, sex/lovemaking/intercourse is not discussed, explored, or a polite topic of conversation. For a fulfilling and satisfying sexual relationship, communication is important, yet many couples find it difficult to talk about sex.

Can you talk to your partner about sex?
Are you comfortable with your sexuality?
Do you know your partner's sexual strategy?

Our attitude, beliefs, and emotions determine our thoughts and feeling about sex. Dysfunctional beliefs can interfere with a healthy, fulfilling, satisfying sexual relationship. If we want to make changes in our lives, we have to recognize, acknowledge, and take ownership of our dysfunctional beliefs and emotions.

200 EFT Tapping Statements for Positive Thinking vs Positive Avoidance

If we keep piling more Band-Aids over a wound, the wound is still there. At some point, the wound needs to be examined, cleaned, and treated in order for heal.

Sometimes it is just "easier" to think positive when we really don't want to look at an issue. Positive Avoidance is denying the truth of a situation. It is a denial of our experience and our feelings about the situation.

When we try to push down our negative emotions, it is like trying to push a ball underwater. The ball pops back up.

Positive Thinking is the act of thinking good or affirmative thoughts, finding the silver lining around a dark cloud, and looking on the more favorable side of an event or condition. It is not denial, avoidance, or false optimism.

Books and Kindles eBooks by Tessa Cason

80 EFT TAPPING STATEMENTS FOR:
Abandonment
Abundance, Wealth, Money
Addictions
Adult Children of Alcoholics
Anger and Frustration
Anxiety and Worry
Change
"Less Than" and Anxiety
Manifesting a Romantic Relationship
Relationship with Self
Self Esteem
Social Anxiety
Weight and Emotional Eating

100 EFT Tapping Statements for Accepting Our Uniqueness and Being Different
100 EFT Tapping Statements for Being Extraordinary!
100 EFT Tapping Statements for Fear of Computers
100 EFT Tapping Statements for Feeling Deserving
100 EFT Tapping Statements for Feeling Fulfilled
200 EFT Tapping Statements for Conflict
200 EFT Tapping Statements for Healing a Broken Heart
200 EFT Tapping Statements for Knowing God
200 EFT Tapping Statements for Positive Thinking vs Positive Avoidance
200 EFT Tapping Statements for Procrastination
200 EFT Tapping Statements for PTSD
200 EFT Tapping Statements for Sex
200 EFT Tapping Statements for Wealth
240 EFT Tapping Statements for Fear
300 EFT Tapping Statements for Healing the Self
300 EFT Tapping Statements for Dealing with Obnoxious People
300 EFT Tapping Statements for Intuition
300 EFT Tapping Statements for Self-defeating Behaviors, Victim, Self-pity
340 EFT Tapping Statements for Healing From the Loss of a Loved One
400 EFT Tapping Statements for Being a Champion
400 EFT Tapping Statements for Being Empowered and Successful
400 EFT Tapping Statements for Dealing with Emotions
400 EFT Tapping Statements for Dreams to Reality
400 EFT Tapping Statements for My Thyroid Story

500 EFT Tapping Statements for Moving Out of Survival
700 EFT Tapping Statements for Weight, Emotional Eating, and Food Cravings
All Things EFT Tapping Manual
Emotional Significance of Human Body Parts
Muscle Testing – Obstacles and Helpful Hints

EFT TAPPING STATEMENTS FOR:
A Broken Heart, Abandonment, Anger, Depression, Grief, Emotional Healing
Anxiety, Fear, Anger, Self Pity, Change
Champion, Success, Personal Power, Self Confidence, Leader/Role Model
Prosperity, Survival, Courage, Personal Power, Success
PTSD, Disempowered, Survival, Fear, Anger
Weight & Food Cravings, Anger, Grief, Not Good Enough, Failure

OTHER BOOKS
Why we Crave What We Crave: The Archetypes of Food Cravings
How to Heal Our Food Cravings

EFT WORKBOOK AND JOURNAL FOR EVERYONE:
Abandonment
Abundance, Money, Prosperity
Addictions
Adult Children of Alcoholics
Anger, Apathy, Guilt
Anxiety/Worry
Being A Man
Being, Doing, Belonging
Champion
Change
Conflict
Courage
Dark Forces
Decision Making
Depression
Difficult/Toxic Parents
Difficult/Toxic People
Emotional Healing

Fear
Forgiveness
God
Grief
Happiness/Joy
Intuition
Leadership
Live Your Dreams
Life Purpose/Mission
People Pleaser
Perfectionism
Personal Power
Relationship w/Others
Relationship w/Self & Commitment to Self
Self Confidence
Self Worth/Esteem
Sex
Shame
Stress
Success
Survival
Transitions
Trust/Discernment
Victim, Self-pity, Self-Defeating Behavior, Shadow Self
Weight and Emotional Eating

Made in the USA
Monee, IL
28 May 2023

34848621R00072